SUB-APOSTOLIC ERA:
Like Wildfire – The Spread of Jesus Way

MUTHIAH APPAVOO

Yesu Avtar Series
XULON PRESS 2013

Copyright © 2013 by Muthiah Appavoo

Sub-Apostolic Era: Like Wildfire–The Spread of Jesus Way
by Muthiah Appavoo

Printed in the United States of America

ISBN 9781626974296

All rights reserved solely by the author. The author guarantees all contents are original and do not infringe upon the legal rights of any other person or work. No part of this book may be reproduced in any form without the permission of the author.

While the primary redaction of the Acts of the Apostles were based on the American Bible Society Contemporary English version (ABS-CEV) © 1995, there are also summaries based on the writings of–Philip Schaff, Ronald Brownrigg, Edgar Goodspeed, B. J. Kidd, J.W.C. Wand and a few others to account for the entire First Century. A bibliography of the books consulted and learned from are listed in the Acknowledgements. The views expressed by the author are not necessarily those of the publisher.

www.xulonpress.com

DEDICATION

Dedicated to Patricia McNeill-Appavoo PhD and her late parents, Lyna-Burkc and Rev. Dr. James McNeill and her late brother, Rev.Dr. John McNeill and my late parents, Sellammal and Rev. Jeeva Wasagam Appavoo and my late brother, Solomon Rajarethnam Appavoo.

TABLE OF CONTENTS

Acknowledgements ix
Foreword: The Rev. Fr. Alwin Hyndman, Old
               Catholic Oratory of Our Lady
               of the Nativity, Port Kells xi
Introduction xiii
Map –   The Spread of Christian Communities
               in the 1st and 2nd Centuries under
               Roman Empire xvii

Part I

Christian Writings during the Century of Lord Jesus
(Sub-Apostolic Era: Like wild fire – Spread of Jesus Way)

Chapter 1   Luke's Premises recording the story
              of the spread of Jesus Way 21
Chapter 2   Out-pouring of the Holy Spirit upon the
              Apostles and the earliest followers of
              Blessed Incarnate Lord Jesus among
              the Hellenistic Jews 25
Chapter 3   Peter and John labour among the Jews
              at Jerusalem & the Jewish Temple 30

Chapter 4	First Challenges to the Apostles from the Jewish hierarchy at Jerusalem– Peter and others pray for courage	.32
Chapter 5	First communal approach to sharing; the sad story of Ananias-Sapphira; unusual power of Peter; troubles for apostles reinforced	.37
Chapter 6	Complaints of the Hellenist followers; and appointment of seven community based administrators	.42
Chapter 7	Stephen's fiery preaching; many conversions among the Hellenists and the stoning of Stephen to death	.45
Chapter 8	Spread of Jesus Way among Samaritan people through Philip and the first convert from non-Jewish proselytes to the Jesus Way- Ethiopian official	48
Chapter 9	Saul the fanatic Jew of Tarsus in Cilicia on the east coast of the Mediterranean	.52
Chapter 10	Peter and Cornelius of Imperial Guard– Jesus message was not of 'particularistic' but of 'universal' significance – Peter learned his lesson the hard way	.57
Chapter 11	Peter's report of the new phenomenon of non-Jewish converts to the community of the "Jesus Way" in Jerusalem and Caesarea	.62
Chapter 12	Herod Antipas I, the grandson of Herod the Great started giving trouble	.65
Chapter 13	Barnabas & Saul sent out with the blessings of the Syrian Antioch Church	.68
Chapter 14	Barnabas and Saul in Iconium and Lystra in the Province of Galatia	.72

Table of Contents

Chapter 15	Jerusalem Jewish Church leaders meet to decide on acceptance of Gentile converts *on par* and gave letters to the evangelists – Saul goes his own way	.76
Chapter 16	Saul heads his own team with Silas and Timothy	.82
Chapter 17	Saul and teams reach out in Thessalonica, Berea in Macedonia and at Athens	.87
Chapter 18	Saul and team visit Corinth and re-visit other places strengthening believers there	.91
Chapter 19	Saul gets into trouble at Ephesus over criticism on many icons prevalent there	.95
Chapter 20	Saul rejects advice of many leaders not to go to Jerusalem due to his convictions	100
Chapter 21	Saul gets to Jerusalem, visits James, gets into the Temple and is arrested	104
Chapter 22	Saul was saved by the Roman commandant at Jerusalem Garrison for protection of Saul from angry mob perhaps stirred up by the Yehudic leadership	109
Chapter 23	The Commandant brought Saul to Jewish Council for trial before a wild crowd	113
Chapter 24	Saul brought before Felix the governor at Caesarea under heavy guard	117
Chapter 25	Saul defends himself in front of Felix & Festus at Caesarea and found not guilty	121
Chapter 26	Agrippa, the great grandson of Herod Great & consort Bernice listen to Saul	124

Chapter 27	Saul's journey to Rome slowed amidst storm and ship-wreck	126
Chapter 28	Saul and party on Island of Malta; ended-up in rental house in Rome	130

Part II

Chapter 29	Life-styles in the First Century Roman Empire and Gentile converts to Jesus Way	137
Chapter 30	Administration, worship, unity and role of apologists, with Church growth	141
Chapter 31	Latin Christianity	150
Chapter 32	A brief note on the activities of the twelve apostles and epilogue prognosis	164

DAILY PRAYERS – Morning, Noon, Evening and Compline 171

BIBLIOGRAPHY 179

Acknowledgements

The 86 years old author and redactor is a retired Anglican priest and a retired Associate Professor of Sociology in the University of Alberta in Edmonton (Concordia College). He has drawn extensively on the writings of many authors found in the Bibliography in his attempts to cover the story of the earliest spread of the message of the followers of the Incarnate Lord Jesus during the First Century, considered as the *Sub-Apostolic Era.*

The writings of particular importance to the author were Ronald Brownrigg (also from which the map was copied); Edgar Goodspeed; B. J. Kidd; Phillip Schaff and J.W.C. Wand. There was no lack of religious literature covering the period. Appavoo was interested in the historical social setting of the events which accompanied the vagaries of the spread of Lord Jesus Way during the sway of the Roman Empire. 'Jew' and 'Yehude' are used interchangeably.

Appavoo owes much to the American Bible Society (ABS) for the Contemporary English Version (CEV) of the New Testament, 1995. He has redacted material from the CEV on the Acts of the Apostles in his own style, skill and sequence and takes responsibility for any errors of judgement in the usage of the CEV text. The tome is not meant to be a sacred text but a simple account of the wild fire like spread of the message of Blessed Lord Jesus.

The author is profoundly grateful to the Reverend Father Alwin Hyndman of the Old Catholic Society Oratory of Our Lady of the Nativity; and for his perusing through the draft manuscript. Father Hyndman had loaned many tomes in the preparation of the manuscript from his Library.

The Right Reverend Trevor Walters, the Suffragan Bishop of Western Canada Diocese of the Anglican Network in Canada, kindly previewed the manuscript and made many suggestions for corrections to the draft manuscript of the Sub-Apostolic Era: Like wild fire spread of the message of Lord Jesus Way. The author found Bishop Walters a very compassionate person.

The map of the extensive areas of the Roman Empire in which the message of Lord Jesus Way was spread during the First and Second centuries of the current era is attached. This was drawn from Ronald Brownrigg' *Twelve Apostles*. Macmillan, 1974, p. 235. The front cover image was drawn from Andre von Grabar's *Die Mittelalterliche Kunst Osteuropas*. Holle Verlag, Baden-Baden 1970, p 61.

The author is grateful to his daughter Clare Appavoo who had helped editing the manuscript prior to forwarding it for non-profit publication. Clare Appavoo is the Executive Director of the Canadian Research and Knowledge Network. The author is blessed in his efforts as Clare had replaced her mother Dr. Patricia Appavoo, who was great in blue penciling draft mss.

The tome is dedicated to the author's spouse Patricia Jean Appavoo, her late parents–Lyna Burke and the Reverend Dr. James McNeill and the author's own late mother Sellammal Devadason and late father the Reverend Jeeva Wasagam Appavoo and his late brother Solomon Rajarethnam Appavoo.

The present tome comes under the **Yesu Avtar** series.

Foreward
Revised insert in place of the original

The Reverend Dr Muthiah David Appavoo has shared with us a condensed, lucid overview of the thought and acts of our forerunners who bolted forth with the Good News! He traces the extraordinary emergence of Christianity in our faith practice, by reflections upon the writings and biographies of the major witnesses who followed on from the Incarnate Lord Jesus Galilean mission and into the first century ad, Sub-Apostolic era. We read of the oral and scripted work of His apostles and their successors and we are touched by their internal conflicts, courageous commitments and insufferable persecutions. Father Appavoo beautifully delivers the texts as they are without formality in a colloquial style.

I have often wished that I had been a student in Professor Appavoo's sociology courses since I for one, have been nurtured as a participating beneficiary of his insight and compassion, his sparkling humour and imagination, his devotion to Sacramental Verities and his concern for the poor in his heritage of India. This priest's smiling rapport with curiosity is so inviting! He savoured the spirituality brought out in the Interfaith study groups which he fostered. He seems to me to crave the type of sharing conversation and fellowship like that enjoined by 'The Inklings'.

Without bringing 'coals to Newcastle', I had to initially acquire a better handle on Muthiah Appavoo's favourite terms: `Yehud' pertaining to Judaism and 'Avatar', a concept of Lord Jesus birth by irruption into this physical world as one of us, an incarnate presence envisioned by some eastern religions yet one that is outside the mindset of Hebrew semetism.

The unfamiliar 'avatara', from Sanskrit, refers to 'descent' in mortals of Divine Incarnation. While this approach to the Divine Word has also been sought by others, paramount to Christians, is the declaration of St John 'et verbum caro factum est'. He did become flesh in the fullness of love which transforms law, guilt and suffering.

Two stimulating aspects I appreciated in this work were Dr Appavoo's extensive research into the details of St Paul's commitment encounters and the plethora of personalities who were instrumental in the wild fire spread of evangelism for Christ; if only such zeal could be realized today!

Can we replicate the first century into the cosmos of century 21? Could there be new and different triggers that would 'shake our foundations' to release a striving for faith so as to affirm a deep spiritual epiphany?

Beginning with the Lord Himself, a band of companion fishermen, a motley collection of curious listeners and the myrrh-bearing women of the Early Primitive Church, discovered a flame burning within their hearts; that was and is the charge ignited in the story of Christ's apostolate. "Where love is, there treasures be; save us all from poverty." I am sure that you will be inspired as I am to share Father Appavoo's insights into the phenomenal discovery of the Lord Jesus Way!

L. Alwin Hyndman +
a priest of the Old Catholic Church of BC
The Oratory of Our Lady of the Nativity Old Catholic Society
Surrey, BC V4N 5X8
Dated: June 28, 2013

Introduction

This is the story of the wild fire like spread of the message of the Blessed Incarnate Lord Jesus (*Yesu Avtar*) during the First Century of the current Era, also considered the **Sub-Apostolic Era.** The message that Lord Jesus gives eternal life was preached among diverse groups of people in an unbelievably short period by the apostles and their disciples. It won the hearts and minds of many people of diverse ethno-cultural heritage, politico-economic status and resident in all parts of the Roman Empire and beyond. The one common element for the most people was the fact that they were part of the Roman Empire. The religious diversity was often unbridgeable.

The early attempt of the twelve apostles and their entourage was to convert the Yehudes, gathered in the synagogues spread all over the coasts of the Mediterranean Sea and availing themselves of the opportunities to address the congregants who were there for prayer and the reading of the Yehudic scriptures and to listen to any homilies provided by any member of the congregation or any Yehudic visitor present. The apostles and their colleagues simply preached that Lord Jesus was indeed the long awaited *great Sage*.

Most present may not have accepted the claims of the apostles and their cohorts. But those who did, spread the claims of the apostles and evangelists to their families, their kin-groups and local communities. The Hellenistic folks more often than not were prepared to accept the claims of the apostles and their followers. By the end of the First Century, many thousands were converted to Lord Jesus Way, besides the 5,000 Jewish respondents at the first challenges made by Stephen the Martyr, Philip the evangelist and the apostles Peter and John. In the following years the apostolic mission trips were made among the cities, towns and villages of the Mediterranean Seaboard, namely the Palestinian territory where the Yehudes and a variety of ethno-cultural groups including the Samaritans were resident. The apostles had earlier decided to divide among themselves the 'global' territories for evangelization.

One of the major follies of the Christian Church was to fall back on Yehudic Law and prophets for their homilies and exegeses. The notes taken down by the earnest disciples of the apostles became later the bases for the Gospels. The Petrine and Pauline epistles and the Apocalypse were incrementally available in hand-written format for use at public worship held in secrecy due to possible persecution. The profound theology that God became human in Jesus from Nazareth who would give new life leading to eternal life was somewhat watered down or even ignored. For the want of new literature, during the Sub-Apostolic Era many early Christian communities often relied on the old Yehudic law and prophets for public reading, as the early Christians still used the synagogue ways of rituals, which Marcion legitimately had challenged. He was strongly impressed by the stories and teachings of love of the Lord Jesus Way. Love was central to Jesus life-style. Alas! Marcion could not prevail in his vision of love and existentialism.

The author has tried to fill the gap between the canonical Acts and the end of the first century with material drawn from other sources. There is a desperate need to learn more about the rest of the apostles and their stories of evangelization in diverse parts of the world. The author believes that there is a need to popularize the stories and teachings of all the apostles and for the entire first century. Polycarp, Justin Martyr and Irenaeus tried to fill the gap and the present author just reiterated the same in an informal, colloquial manner. The historical Eucharistic theology needed reassertion.

Appavoo has known how hard, difficult and risky it could be to speak forth of the message of the Blessed Lord Jesus among diverse religious communities in the 1940s through mid-1960s. His families had suffered in centuries gone by. The author, his father, cousin, paternal and maternal grand fathers and an aunt were engaged in pastoral assignments and had known a little about the antagonisms and even violence when it came to caring for the under-class/caste folks. The author praises the Lord for all His tender mercies, support, strength and guidance.

There were times of joy preaching at evangelistic gatherings and tent missions, mainly at the Youth for Christ tent missions in a few provinces/States in India and in Deutschland in the 1950s. There were many wonderful occasions of leading a few adults and youth to commitment to the Blessed Incarnate Lord Jesus as their saviour and Lord.

The pastoral ministry in Bangalore, India involved providing care, prayer and transport support, on a day-to-day basis. Such care often included sick visitation at the family level and at the hospitals. The author praises God for the health care provided by Christian and other religious physicians, nurses and other care-providers in hospitals and clinics.

The joys one experienced in India was the openness of public hospitals for people of all social status. Most of the time, all such care was provided freely. People of wealth could access for their healthcare needs in privately funded clinics and hospitals. The author's past experiences of care provided at the Christian mission hospitals were of equal merit. Compassion and love seemed to prevail among the healthcare professionals.

Please refer to Muthiah Appavoo. *Memoir* and *Yesu Avtar* as well)

Introduction

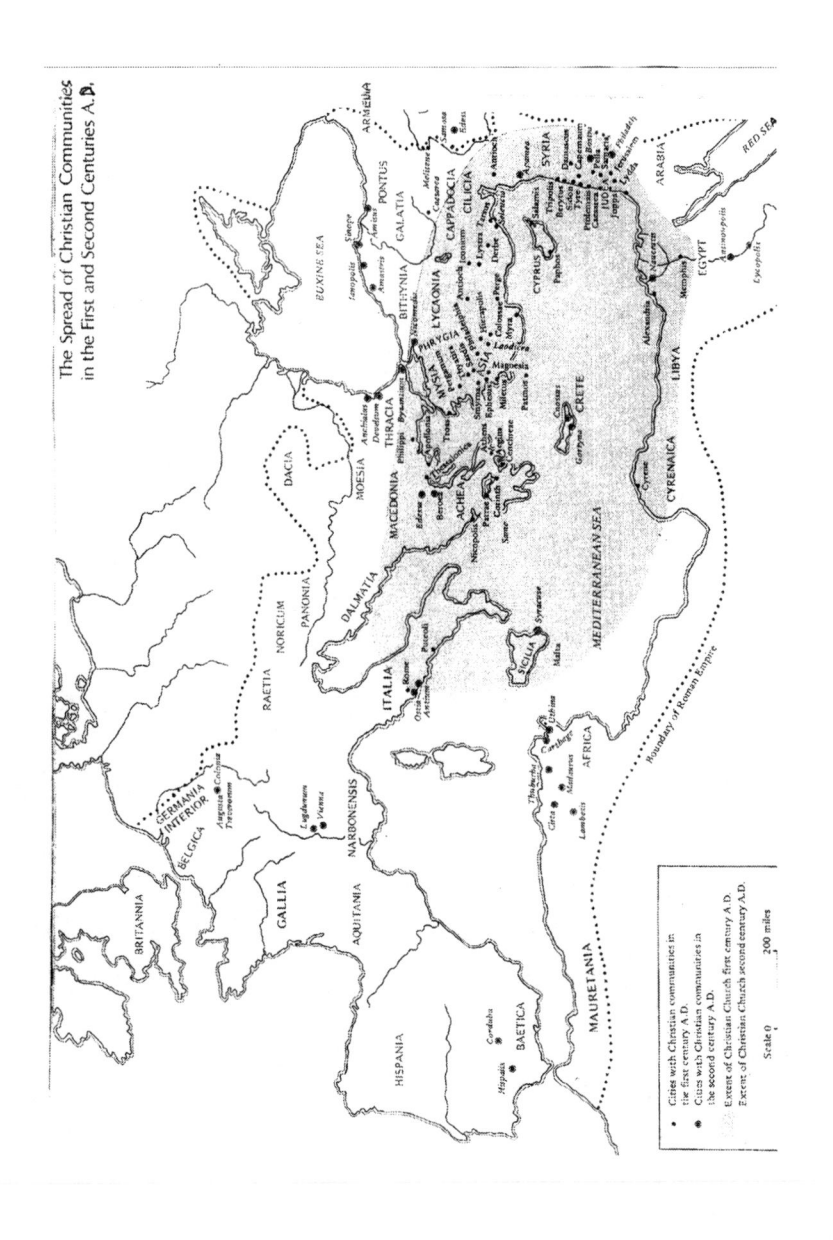

WRITINGS OF THE CENTURY OF OUR LORD JESUS

Sub-Apostolic Era:

Like wild fire — the Spread of Jesus Way

PART I

Christian writings during the century of Lord Jesus

(Sub-Apostolic Era: Like wild fire–The spread of Jesus Way)

ACTS 1

Luke's Premises recording the story of the spread of Jesus Way

Luke, a disciple of Saul and a follower of Lord Jesus wrote the Gospel of Luke addressed to Theophilus of equestrian rank. The second account of the early spread of the Jesus Way was also addressed to the same person, who may have been deprived of his rank since his conversion to Jesus Way. In the Acts, Luke begins by reiterating about all that Jesus did and taught from the very first until Jesus ascension. But before Jesus was taken up, he had given his chosen apostles some detailed instructions with the help of the Holy Spirit.

The Lord had in diverse ways interacted with his disciples and reinforced their faith in Him for forty days after his suffering and death. Jesus had been proving in many ways that he had been raised from death. During his appearances to his disciples, the Lord talked of the wider scope and the persuasive power of the God's Kingdom among human kind.

During the appearances to his apostles Jesus spoke about God's kingdom.

Jesus had urged his faint-hearted disciples to await their empowerment by the gift of the Holy Spirit. He specifically instructed the apostles and the intimate circle of followers to stay together in the place they often met. He told them not to leave Jerusalem but to wait where they were residing till the Father endued them with the Holy Spirit, just as he had foretold them of the Father's promise. John the Baptist was preparing his followers with a baptism of water. But Jesus had promised that in a few days they would be anointed with the outpouring of the Holy Spirit.

- Jesus was taken to Heaven

While the apostles were still with the post-resurrected Lord Jesus, they were interested primarily, in the overthrow of the Roman dominance. The idea of Yehudic quest for the overthrow of the Roman yoke, which was the reality since BC63 Pompeii invasion and control of Judaea was so deeply rooted in their psyche. They enquired whether Jesus would be willing and ready to overthrow the mighty Roman empire that the Yehudes might achieve their dreams of regaining their political goals. Jesus response was one of affirming that the Father had kept secret his plans. They did not need to know the times and events that only the Father controlled, rather that the Holy Spirit would come upon them and give them spiritual energy and authority. Only then would they be empowered to proclaim about Jesus and his message everywhere in the world, including Jerusalem, Judaea and Samaria.

After Jesus had spoken in this manner and while they were watching (*on the Mount of Olives*), he was taken up into a cloud. They could not see him any more, but they kept on looking up into the sky. Suddenly two men dressed in white clothes were standing there beside them. They had enquired as to why the Galileans were standing there and looking up into the sky? Jesus had been taken up to heaven. But he would come back in the same way they had seen him go.

- Someone to take the place of Judas

The apostles who had been present at the Mount of Olives when Jesus was taken up to the Heavens were Peter, John, James, Andrew, Philip, Thomas, Bartholomew, Matthew, James the son of Alphaeus, Simon, known as the Eager One, and Judas the son of James.

[Under the dominance of the Roman Empire since 63BC, there was often tension among the devout and somewhat overly zealous Jewish folk. They were later named Zealots. At least four of the twelve disciples of the Lord could be considered to be 'Zealots' yet they were faithful to Jesus through his sufferings, crucifixion, and death. Obviously, they were justified as Jesus had been resurrected and guided and ennobled them to be faithful to the end.]

After the apostles returned to the city, they went upstairs to the room where they had been gathering regularly, perhaps at John Mark's home. The apostles often met together for prayer with a single purpose in mind. The devout women and Mary the mother of Jesus would meet with them, and so would Jesus brothers *(perhaps they were his step-brothers or cousins)*.

One day there were about one hundred and twenty of the Lord's followers meeting together, and Peter assuming authority, stood up to speak to them. He suggested that since Judas Iscariot had already committed suicide they had to find a replacement. Peter had cautioned that their choice of replacement should be one who had been with the Lord's followers from the time the Lord Jesus was baptized by John until the day he had been taken to heaven.

Two men were suggested: one was Joseph Barsabbas, also popularly known as Justus, and the other was Matthias. Then they all prayed to the Lord who knew what everyone was like! They asked the Lord to show them the one He had chosen to be an apostle and to serve in place of Judas Iscariot. They had cast a ballot and drew the name of Matthias. He joined the group of the eleven apostles with prayer and the laying on of hands by the other apostles and leaders.

ACTS 2

Outpouring of the Holy Spirit upon apostles and earliest followers of blessed incarnate Lord Jesus among the Hellenistic Jews

On the day of Pentecost, which was fifty days after the Passover (*harvest festival*), all the Lord's followers were assembled together. Unexpectedly, they experienced a blast of a storm. It was a very peculiar sound, which filled the house. Then the Lord's followers had envisioned what appeared to be fiery tongues circulating among the followers which settled on every body. It was the Holy Spirit taking possession of everyone present. The followers of the Lord started speaking in the diverse languages recognizable as the mother tongues of the Yehudes who were either residents in and around Jerusalem or were visitors from elsewhere in the Roman Empire.

Many devout, Hellenized Yehudes were present in Jerusalem for the Feast of Pentecost. When they heard the powerful sound of the blast of a storm, a crowd gathered around those who were in-filled with the power of the Holy Spirit. The crowd was surprised, because they were hearing everything in their own languages. There was excitement and amazement amongst the crowd. Those who became disciples of Jesus queried how the fishermen, who were primarily uneducated Galilean fishermen, could be speaking in the diverse languages of the crowd. Those present at the Feast of Pentecost came from Parthia, Media, Elam, Mesopotomia, Judaea, Cappodocia, Pontus, West Asia, Phrygia, Pamphylia, Egypt, parts of Libya near Cyrene, Rome, Crete, and Arabia. Some of them were born Jews, and others were proselytes to Judaism. They wondered aloud about God's favour!

There was amazement and confusion. Some of them, in sympathy, asked one another about the newly found linguistic skills and knowledge of the apostles and their friends. There were others who made fun of the Lord's followers and exclaimed that they may be drunk!

- Peter Speaks to the Crowd

Peter the leader stood-up with the eleven apostles around him and spoke-up in a loud but clear voice to the crowd and addressed them as friends as well as those who lived in Jerusalem and its environs. Peter wanted the assembled crowd to pay attention to what he had to say. They were wrong to consider that the people who were rejoicing and praising God were drunk. It was only nine in the morning!

Peter reminded the crowd that God had foretold their ancestors that in the days to come, the Holy Spirit would in-fill every one; that their sons and daughters would exhort them to turn to the Lord, that their young men would experience visions and that their older men would dream of great things. God had promised to give his Spirit to both men and women, and they would bear bold witness. There would be miraculous events in the sky above and the earth beneath. On that wonderful 'day of the Lord' God would have granted the wishes of those who had asked for his help.

[The concept of the 'Day of the Lord' was very prevalent among the Jewish people of Judaea and Jerusalem in particular. They were conquered by the Roman General Pompeii in 63 BC and were annexed to the Roman Empire as one of the many provinces. The Governor was at Caesarea and a procurator was located at the Roman garrison at Jerusalem. The Jewish and the Samaritan people had to pay taxes and customs duties to the Romans. Some of the Yehudic religious fanatics (*Pharisees*) were resentful and sometimes revolted against the dominance and corruption of the Roman officialdom. 'The Day of the Lord' was seen as immanent towards freedom from the Roman yoke. Blessed Lord Jesus was not too concerned about it. His *modus operandi* was redemption towards eternal life. Earthly freedom from the Roman yoke was not the paramount issue for Lord Jesus. The Yehudic leadership decided on putting Him to death as He was attracting many followers and it would have been counter-productive to the Pharisaic and even the wealthy Sadducees' cause.]

Peter pressed on by pleading with the crowd to hear him regarding what he had to say about Jesus from Nazareth. God had proved that he sent his Son Jesus for their benefit through His works of miracles, wonders, and signs. All of them had known about what took place in recent days. Peter preached that it was in fulfillment of God's plan that Lord Jesus had come. They, who benefitted from Jesus words and works, handed him over to be put to death by crucifixion by the Roman regime.

[The truth was that at the instigation of the Jerusalem Jewish leaders, Jesus had been put to death by the Roman procurator who in fact had no desire to shed the blood of an innocent person.]

The wonderful thing about the trial and death of Lord Jesus was, He had been resurrected! Death had no power over Lord Jesus. God did not let Lord Jesus' body decay, as Jesus had risen again from the grave.

Peter had gone on to reassert that all of the followers of Lord Jesus could tell the crowd unequivocally that God had raised Jesus to life! Jesus had ascended to the heavens to sit at the right side (*the place of honour and power*) of God. At his baptism by John, God the Father had given Lord Jesus the Holy Spirit. Jesus was also the one who had given the Holy Spirit to all of them at the Feast of Pentecost, which they were just then watching and/or, hearing about. Peter asserted that everyone amongst the Jews should have known for certain that God had made Jesus both Lord and saviour, even though they had put him to death on a cross.

When the people had heard Peter's exhortation, they were very disturbed. They had asked Peter and the other apostles what they should have been doing. Peter had responded by inviting them to turn around and believe in Lord Jesus; and then to be baptized in His Name. Then they too would have experienced the power of Lord Jesus and had been freed from guilt of their sins. They and their close kin would also be given the Holy Spirit, no matter where they had lived.

Peter had advised them of many other matters in response to their queries. He had urged the assembled crowd to save themselves from what awaited all evil people. Following Peter's exhortation, about three thousand Jewish people believed his message and were baptized. They spent much time listening to and learning from the apostles. Those who put their faith in Lord Jesus were like family to one another. They had shared food together and often celebrated the Lord's Supper and had prayed together.

[It was most likely that the crowd that listened to Peter were the Hellenistic Yehudes visiting Jerusalem for the Feast of Pentecost. The Jerusalem Jews were either the fanatical Pharisees or, the Sadducees who were part of the establishment aligned with the Roman Empire. The Sadducees were fairly well off financially and were in control of the Jerusalem temple treasury.]

- Life-styles among the followers of Lord Jesus

People were amazed by the many miracles and wonders that the apostles performed. All the Lord's followers met together frequently and had shared everything they had. Some had sold their property and possessions and had given the money to whoever had need. Day after day they had fellowship together in the temple. Many of the Jewish people prayed in their homes at regular times each day. The Lord's followers had come together in different homes and had shared their food happily and freely, while praising God. Everyone liked them; and each day the Lord added to their group as others who were being saved joined them. They celebrated the Lord's Supper in various homes to avoid persecution.

[It was impossible to be followers of Lord Jesus and not be persecuted, if the Roman procurator or governor decided to take action. One may query why the Roman governor or the garrison commander had tolerated the apostles and the other followers of the Lord. Perhaps they were considered as part of the Jerusalem Jewish establishment. They were seen as a sectarian movement among the constantly rebellious Yehudes. The followers of the Lord were ignored as their numbers did not warrant action. The Jerusalem Jews had not yet risen up in revolt against the followers of Lord Jesus. When Jesus was alive and was gaining popularity, the Pharisees and to some extent the establishment Sadducees saw to it that he would be put to death. They did not believe He would rise again. But He did. Rome ignored the claims of the resurrection of Jesus as bogus. Life went on as the Roman garrison at Jerusalem had enough on their hands not to be bothered with some religious and ideological claims.]

ACTS 3

Peter and John labour among the Yehudes at Jerusalem and the Jewish temple

Peter and John had decided to attend the Three-o-clock afternoon daily prayers at the Jerusalem Temple. Just as in all temples during ancient times, there were many sick and poor present at the temple looking for alms. One such person was carried daily to the side of the door known as the Beautiful Gate. He was born-lame and had begged for alms from the people who were entering the door. When he saw Peter and John about to enter the temple, he begged for money.

Peter and John had stared straight at him and asked him to look at them. He was encouraged and expected to get some coins. Peter pointed out that he had no silver or gold coins. He would do for him what he could. Peter commanded that in the name of Lord Jesus of Nazareth, he should get up and walk. So saying, Peter gave the beggar his right hand and helped him up.

The feet and ankles of the person became strong. He jumped up and started walking. He followed Peter and John into the temple, walking and jumping and praising God. All the people who had witnessed the event started praising God. They were totally astonished! They could not imagine what had happened to the man.

- Peter speaks in the Jerusalem Temple

The man clung to Peter and John. The crowd, which had witnessed the event ran towards them at the public place known as Solomon's porch along the east side of the temple. Peter saw an opportune moment to witness to the blessed Lord Jesus and in a loud and clear voice addressed them as friends and enquired if they had been overawed by what they had witnessed. He exhorted that he and John were not the ones who had healed the man. He asked rhetorically if they thought it was their piety that helped heal the man. No! Peter said emphatically that it was not. Rather, Peter continued that God had sent Lord Jesus for the Jewish people's healing but they had rejected him and handed him over to the Roman regime to put him to death, in spite of the fact that Pontius Pilate, the Roman procurator at Jerusalem, had found no guilt in Jesus and wished to free him. The Yehudic leadership and the street mob rejected a holy and good person and had asked for a murderer to be set free instead. They had killed the one who led people to life.

All the apostles would have borne witness to what Jesus had done for the lame man. The Yehudic crowd surely had known the lame man. He put his faith in the name of Jesus and his limbs became strong. The man's Faith in Jesus lead to his healing, while everyone was watching.

ACTS 4

First Challenges to the apostles from the Jewish hierarchy at Jerusalem – Peter and others pray for courage

- Peter and John were brought before the Jerusalem Jewish Council

The message got to the Temple priests and the hierarchy. While Peter was still talking and answering questions from the crowd, some of the priests, the captain of the temple guard, and some Sadducees arrived. The Sadducees were furious because the apostles were proclaiming that the dead would be resurrected just as Jesus was raised from death and decay.

It was already late in the afternoon. The Council had decided to arrest both Peter and John and to keep them in the local jail-cell for the night. This did not stop the people from believing in Jesus based on what Peter and John had proclaimed. As a result of Peter's message and the presence of the Holy Spirit, there were about five thousand who had become the followers of the Lord.

The leaders, elders, and the scribes (*lawyers*) met in Jerusalem, the next morning. The high priest Annas as well as Caiaphas, John, Alexander, and other members of the high priest's family (*clan*) were present. The jailer brought in Peter and John and made them stand in the middle of the Council chamber, while the Council queried Peter and John regarding their authority and in whose name they had carried out the healing of the lame beggar.

Being filled with the Spirit of God, Peter challenged the assembled leaders about what they were charging the two apostles regarding a good deed done in which a lame man was made whole. They had news for the Yehudic priests and the crowd. The man who was standing there in their midst was totally healed because of the power of Jesus of Nazareth, whom they had put to death. God resurrected him to life and He had ascended to heaven.

Only Jesus had the power to heal. There was no other Name in the world, by which anyone could be made whole (*both in body and Spirit*). The leaders were astounded to hear how well they spoke and how brave they were. They were well aware of the fact that both the apostles Peter and John were only ordinary men and not well educated. They knew however, that the two had been with Jesus.

They could not deny what had happened to the cripple as he was standing alongside of the two apostles. The leaders had asked the two to leave the council room. Then the officials discussed a strategy to stop further activity by the apostles. They were were wondering what they could do about it.

Everyone in Jerusalem would soon come to hear about the miraculous healing of the lame beggar; denying it happened was pointless. The Jewish leaders were concerned that such kind of wondrous acts be stopped from spreading any further. They proposed one strategy; to give the apostles dire warnings and to threaten them not to speak to anyone about the name of Jesus. On this strategy, all were agreed; and they called the two apostles back in and threatened them with dire consequences should they teach in the name of Jesus.

The response from Peter and John was a challenge to the hierarchy, *viz.*, that they could not obey the commands of human leaders which opposed God's commands. Nobody could deny what they had seen and heard (*i.e., the life and times with Jesus of Nazareth*)

The Council could not find any excuse to punish Peter and John for their healing action. The leaders simply warned the two apostles and let them go. The man who was miraculously healed was over forty, and everyone praised God for what had happened.

[Even in ancient times there was scope for 'freedom of expression' and noble actions, which often could be substituted with new laws nowadays.]

- Peter and others pray for courage to proclaim Jesus

After Peter and John had been let go by the Sanhedrin, they got back to the Lord's followers and reiterated all that happened to them at the Sanhedrin. When the rest of the Lord's followers heard about what had happened, they felt somewhat triumphant that the apostles had survived their first test. Immediately, they organized times of prayer together calling on God who had created heaven and earth, the sea, and everything in them. By the Holy Spirit, He had spoken in the past about the coming Saviour.

Herod Antipater, the son of Herod the Great and Pontius Pilate had teamed up with the Gentiles and the Yehudic multitude. Then they turned against God's holy Son Jesus, the saviour so destined. The apostles and their followers prayed to the Lord, earnestly beseeching him to protect them from the fury and dire threats of the Jerusalem Yehudic hierarchy!

The apostles were the servants of the Lord. They prayed for courage to be bold, to speak out about the Lord's message. They earnestly prayed to the Lord to make known His mighty power that the apostles might continue to heal people and engage in wondrous actions in the name of Lord Jesus His Son.

Just as they had earnestly prayed for God's power to continue with them, their meeting place shook. They were all filled with the Holy Spirit and were emboldened to proclaim the message.

- Sharing of possessions among the Lord's followers

The idea of communal life-style became popular among the group of followers of Lord Jesus. Their thinking about everything was also in harmony. Ideally, wealth and personal possessions were replaced by community caring and sharing approach. They shared all possessions in common and there were no claims to individualistic rights to riches and material wealth.

In an emphatic way the apostles maintained that Lord Jesus was alive. People who had witnessed the life-styles of the followers of Lord Jesus respected them. God had honoured the followers of Lord Jesus. Nobody went without their needs being met. All this was done in a voluntary manner. Many who had legally owned land or houses often sold them and brought the money to the apostles. In turn, the apostles and other leaders would provide financial and other assistance to the needy. Joseph Barnabas (i.e., *one who encourages others*) was one such person from Cyprus who sold a piece of his property and brought the money to the apostles.

[Michael Greene in his *Evangelism in the Early Church* (p.235f) had seen the strategic value of the Synagogues in the spread of the message of Jesus Way. All members and visitors of Jewish background had opportunity to read in public the Jewish scriptures and address the community gathered for worship and prayer. The approach needed to be conciliatory, sympathetic to the susceptibilities of the gathered community; courage in openly recognizing any problems in presenting truths which were opposed vehemently by some of the hearers; genuine respect for the hearers; and trust in the power of the gospel of Lord Jesus. This applied also to open-air preaching. There were also exhortations in the manner of a *Sage,* which benefitted the hearers as they judged such exhortations as pertinent for themselves.]

ACTS 5

First communal approach to sharing; the sad story of Ananias-Sapphira; Peter's Unusual power; trouble for apostles reinforced

- Peter's fierce condemnation of Ananias and Sapphira

There was a couple who became the followers of the Lord, Ananias and Sapphira a fairly well off pair. Following the example of others, they too decided to sell a parcel of their property to give to the apostles for distribution to the needy. Unfortunately, they decided to keep behind some of the sale price for their own purposes. Hence Ananias and Sapphira colluded in their attempt at lying to the apostles about the sale-price.

[It was possible that Ananias and Sapphira had wished to be seen as liberal in their gift, that they had given all of their sale-value, hence the attempt at a little lie.]

Ananias came in first and brought the reduced sale-value. Peter saw through the lie and challenged him as to why he had let Shaithan (*Satan*) make him lie to the Holy Spirit. The property was his and he did not have to give a portion of the sale price and pretend that the amount Ananias had brought in was the sale-price. He had not lied to the people. He had lied to God. When Ananias heard Peter's admonition, he dropped down dead. Everyone who heard about what had happened was frightened. Some young men who were present came up and wrapped the body of Ananias and took it out and buried it.

Sapphira came in about three hours later, not knowing what had happened to her husband. Peter asked Sapphira as to whether she and her husband had sold their property for the amount they had claimed. She affirmed that it was the sale price.

Then Peter spoke up peremptorily charging why she and her husband had colluded to test the Lord's Spirit. Peter continued his accusations by pointing out that the men who had buried Ananias were by the door, and they would carry her out as well. Hearing Peter's verdict, she too fell down at Peter's feet and died. When the young men came back, they saw the body of Sapphira. So, they carried her out and buried her beside her husband.

When the recently baptized members of the Jerusalem believers in Lord Jesus saw or heard what took place they were terrified, and so was everyone else who heard about what had happened.

- Peter's unusual power as the lead apostle

The apostles worked many miracles and wonders among the people. All of the Lord's followers often met in the hall of the temple, known as Solomon's Porch. Many worshipers at the temple did not dare to go to that hall for fear of raising the ire of the Yehudic hierarchy. However, it was also a fact that many Jerusalem temple folks put their faith in Lord Jesus. People carried their sick on cots and mats to the roadside where the apostles, especially Peter might pass by, in the hopes that their shadow might cure the sick. Many people who lived in the suburbia also brought their sick and the mentally ill and they were all healed.

- Trouble for the apostles

It was from among the Sadducees that the high priests were selected. They controlled the day-to-day priestly functions. They and their clan became extremely jealous of what the apostles were doing. They decided to arrest the apostles and put them in the city jail. An angel from God opened the doors to the jail and led the apostles out. The angel instructed the apostles to return to the temple and carry on their teaching about the new-life through Lord Jesus. Back they went into the temple before sunrise and started teaching. Obviously, there were crowds still around who were willing to listen to the apostles preaching and teaching!

The high priest got together his Council along with other Yehudic leaders. The Council had asked the jailer to bring out the apostles. The temple police who were sent to the jail did not find the apostles. They returned and reported that the jail doors were locked and the guards were at their posts. When the temple police opened the doors and went in, they did not find any body there. The captain of the temple police and the chief priests heard about this but they did not know what to make of the strange escapes.

Someone came into the Council meeting and reported that the folk who were imprisoned were just then in the temple preaching and teaching the people! The captain (*i.e., the chief constable!*) went with a squad of his men and brought the apostles back without use of any force for fear of being stoned by the people.

The frustrated high priest accused the apostles that he had strictly instructed them not to preach and teach in the name of Jesus, yet they disobeyed his command and their actions may have had repercussions. The high priest pointed out to the apostles that by their teaching all over Jerusalem about Jesus, the priest were blamed for Jesus death!

It was Peter who responded to the high priest's complaint. He retorted that the apostles did not obey people over against God's commands. The Yehudic hierarchy were the ones who had killed Jesus by handing him over to the Roman procurator, Pilot, demanding that Lord Jesus be put to death by crucifixion. They forced the hands of Pilot.

The God who Yehudes worshipped had resurrected Jesus to life making him their Leader and Saviour. Then, Lord Jesus ascended to the heavens and sat at God's right hand side. It was God's intention that the Yehudic folk would turn to him and be forgiven and experience freedom. The apostles were just reiterating about the risen and ascended Lord Jesus! The Holy Spirit was God's gift to everyone who obeyed God. When the Council members heard those bold words from Peter, they became so angry that they wished to kill the apostles then and there. One of the assembled Council members was the learned and highly respected teacher Gamaliel. He persuaded the Council to get the apostles out of the room for a few minutes.

When they were sent out, Gamaliel warned the Council that they had better be careful as to what they did with those men. They should recall that not so long ago Theudas claimed to be someone important, and about four hundred men joined with him. Theudas mutinied and was put to death. All his companions were scattered away, and that was the end of the movement. There was a similar episode of rebellion. When the Romans took census of the Yehudic people, Judas from Galilee showed up in his efforts at getting rid of the Roman yoke. A lot of people followed Judas, but he was also killed, and his followers were scattered.

Gamaliel went on to ask the Council to stay away from the apostles. His advice was to leave them alone. If what they taught were something of their own new ideology, it might fail. However, if God was guiding them, the Council could not stop them anyway, unless they wanted to fight against God. The Council members heeded the advice of Gamaliel and called the apostles back in. They had the apostles whipped and gave dire warnings not to speak in the name of Jesus and let them go.

After they were let go, the apostles were joyful and felt that God was with them and considered them worthy enough to suffer for the sake of Jesus. Every day the apostles spent time in the temple; and in one home or another of the followers of Lord Jesus. They never stopped preaching and teaching the Yehudes of Jerusalem and the Hellenists and telling the good news that Jesus was indeed the Son of God.

ACTS 6

Complaints of the Hellenist followers; and appointment of seven community based Administrators

- The Church chooses seven administrative leaders

The apostles had proclaimed the new life, which Lord Jesus gave. Many people had become followers of the Lord at Jerusalem. It was customary to provide daily food supplies to the poor widows. There arose some complaint that while the Aramaic speaking poor were daily provided with food and other necessities, the Greek speaking poor were neglected.

The twelve apostles called all the followers together and reasoned with them that they had to continue with their preaching God's message and not to become entangled in the administration and in helping charitable activities.

[Perhaps, the daily food subsidies also functioned as an informal banking service]

Peter assumed his leadership role and called upon the needy to choose from among themselves seven honourable and wise men filled with the Holy Spirit. The apostles would be prepared to prayerfully approve them to attend to the day-to-day administrative roles. Thus the apostles could continue with prayer and preaching the work of God.

Peter's suggestion pleased everyone; and they began by choosing Stephen, a man of great faith and a great evangelist and filled with the Holy Spirit. Then they had decided on the apostle Philip, a practical and selfless man. They also recommended Prochorus, Nicanor, Timon, Parmenas, and Nicolaus. Nicholas was a Jewish convert at Antioch. They were presented to the apostles who prayed over them and laid their hands on them to signify that they were approved for the administrate duties. Freed from administrative roles, the apostles concentrated their efforts on evangelism. Consequently, God's message was made known to many more people in Jerusalem; and many put their faith in Lord Jesus including many of the priests.

- Arrest of Stephen the Deacon

Stephen the evangelist was endued with power to perform wondrous miracles among the people. Some of the 'freed-men' (*i.e., men who were former slaves but worked their way to freedom*) were unimpressed. Those freed-men Jews from Cyrene and Alexandria started arguing with Stephen. Some of the other freed-men from Cilicia and Asia also joined in the melee. All of those challengers were discomfited by Stephen who had spoken with great persuasion and authority granted by the Holy Spirit. The freed-men therefore decided upon devious means to vilify Stephen. They talked some folks into lying by saying that they had heard Stephen saying terrible things against the Jewish Laws and God. Then they dragged him before the Sanhedrin (*i.e., the Jerusalem Jewish Council*).

Those who agreed to tell lies about Stephen alleged that Stephen was saying terrible things about their holy temple and the ancient Jewish-Laws; Stephen had claimed that Jesus from Nazareth was going to destroy the temple and change the ritual and customs of ancient times.

All the Council members looked intently at Stephen. They had noticed that Stephen's face shone like that of an angel.

ACTS 7

Stephen's fiery preaching; many conversions among the Hellenists and the stoning to death of Stephen

- **Stephen's powerful speech**

In response to the high priest's challenge as to whether the complaint against him was valid, Stephen responded regaling with history lessons on the Yehudic clans taking 'possession' of the Hittite, Hivite, Jebusite and Moab territories in ancient times till they established themselves with Jerusalem as their capitol. As for the fate of all their own Jewish leaders, they were all harassed or, murdered.

Their Temple at Jerusalem was loaded with precious stones and gold and silver. Alas! The Jews were made captive by the Babylonians who had invaded them and took many of their well-educated and rich folks. When they returned to the land in which they were originally settled, they brought back with them many of the behavioural norms of the Babylonians including their rituals.

When the returned captives had rebuilt their temple, for a while they enjoyed peace and prosperity. Some of the devout were patiently waiting for a powerful *Sage* to appear and relieve the Yehudic people from the yoke of foreign domination.

[Unfortunately for the Jewish nation, as stated earlier on, when the Roman general Pompeii had swept through both Judaea and Samaria in BC63, the Roman laws and behavioural norms held sway. Rome let the local customs and traditions continue to a large extent, as long they were not antithetical to the interests of the Empire, which included colonial taxation and revenue sharing. It is possible that the 'Babylonian captivity' referred to the area which was described as 'Judah' which the Babylonian Empire had over-run and turned it into one of its provinces. Perhaps Pompeii in 63 BC had conquered that province of Babylonia as well]

Stephen did not mince his words. He called the Yehudic high priest and his cohort as stubborn and hard headed persons! They were always fighting against the Holy Spirit; and by Stephen's days they had murdered the kindly and good Son of God, Lord Jesus, who was sent among them to be their spiritual saviour.

Lord Jesus was never into any power trips. He was the humblest of the humble. He had gone about doing good for the people, healing their sick and the mentally ill. He even raised to life the dead. The Yehudic people of Judaea, as mentioned before, were determined to hang on to power. They had their own internal splits – Aramaic speaking Pharisees, Hellenistic wealthy high priests and their colleagues. They could not bear to put up with Lord Jesus and his acts of love and peace. They had him put to death, but God raised him to life and he ascended to heaven and was by at the right side of God the Father.

- Stephen Stoned to Death

Stephen's oratorical accusations made the Jerusalem Council members angry, even furious. Stephen standing in the midst of the Council looked up towards the beyond and being filled with the power of the Holy Spirit exclaimed that he envisioned the heavens opened and the glorious God and Jesus standing at his right hand-side. The council members were aghast and covered their ears. In their fury, the priestly leaders and the crowd began to throw stones at Stephen. Then they dragged Stephen out of the city walls and proceeded with their further attacks. The men who had accused Stephen laid their outerwear at the feet of Saul a learned young Pharisee and a student of Gamaliel. As Stephen was stoned to death, he cried out praying to Lord Jesus, to let him in to His presence. Stephen also pleaded with Lord Jesus not to lay the blame on the incensed men for what they were doing to him. Stephen died of the wounds. Some followers of the Lord took a risk and buried Stephen and mourned much for him. However, Saul the new one on the scene approved of Stephen being stoned to death.

ACTS 8

Spread of Jesus Way among Samaritan people through Philip and the first convert from non-Jewish proselytes to Jesus Way – Ethiopian official

- Saul makes trouble for the Church

All of the Lord's followers, except the apostles, under diverse persecution were scattered everywhere in Judaea, Galilee and Samaria. The newly emerging church came under attack. The fanatically disposed Saul was determined to eliminate the budding church, the followers of Lord Jesus. Saul had the support of the Yehudic leadership and he was relentless in his search for the followers of the Lord by going house to house and putting the followers into jail.

- The Good News was preached in Samaria

Even under attack and being scattered throughout Judaea and Samaria, the Lord's followers went from place to place, talking of Lord Jesus Way. Philip the evangelist went to the city of Samaria and told the people there about Lord Jesus. The Samaritans gathered around Philip to hear him out as well as witness the miracles Philip was performing. Many of the Samaritans who were afflicted with mental disorders (*evil spirits*) became well again. Sometimes, the evil spirits screamed before leaving the possessed. Many who were crippled or lame became well. All the Samaritan citizens who had witnessed the powerful work of Philip were glad over what blessings came their way.

There lived in Samaria a magician named Simon who had gained the approbation of the Samaritans through his performance of magic. He used witchcraft to gain popularity among the rich and the poor, who were always crowding around him. The people thought that Simon was 'the great power.' This went on for a long time. When the people believed what Philip was saying about Lord Jesus Way, they were all baptized. Simon the magician also believed and was baptized. He stayed close to Philip, because he marvelled at all the miracles and wonders.

The apostles in Jerusalem were made aware of how the Samaritans were accepting Lord Jesus Way; Peter and John were sent to learn more about what was taking place in Samaria.

When the two apostles arrived, they prayed that the people would be given the Holy Spirit. The apostles realized that the Holy Spirit was not given to anyone in Samaria, although some of them had been baptized in the name of Lord Jesus. Peter and John decided to lay their hands on everyone who had faith in the Lord, and they received the Holy Spirit.

Now Simon the magician was a keen observer. He noticed that the Spirit was given only when the apostles placed their hands on the people. So he brought money and requested Peter and John to let him have the power to place his hands on people that they might be given the Holy Spirit.

Peter's response was that Simon was sadly mistaken. He could not buy God's gifts through money and that Simon did not have any part in the efforts of the apostles. God knew that Simon the magician's heart was not in harmony with

God. He had to get rid of his evil thoughts and ask God for forgiveness. Peter had realized that jealousy also played a role in Simon's evil ways. Simon the magician begged Peter to pray to the Lord on his behalf that no evil might come to pass.

Peter and John retuned to Jerusalem after their preaching tour in Samaria. On their way back they spoke of the good news of Lord Jesus in all the Samaritan villages.

- Philip and an Ethiopian official

An angel of the Lord had spoken to Philip the apostle and evangelist instructing him to travel south about noon hour, along the desert road which led from Jerusalem to Gaza in the desert. Philip followed the angelic instructions. There, the chief treasurer of the Queen of Ethiopia, a God-fearer (i.e., a *non-Yehude convert to Yehudism*) was returning from Jerusalem where he had been for worship. He was reading aloud from the book of Isaiah as he was riding along the desert road in his chariot. Philip was urged by the Spirit to catch up with the chariot. As Philip caught up with the chariot he could hear the words of the passage the official was reading. Philip enquired of the Ethiopian official whether he could follow what he was reading.

The official had replied that unless somebody familiar with the text could help him, he could not comprehend. He then invited Philip to come up and sit beside him. The passage was from the *Sage* Isaiah which stated that he was led like a sheep on its way to be sacrificed and that he was silent as a lamb whose wool was being sheared and that he was quiet. He was treated in a demeaning manner and that there was no fair trial.

The official had asked Philip as to whether the *Sage* was self-reflecting or, was he referring to someone else.

Here came the opportunity for Philip to explain the passage leading to the message of Lord Jesus.

As they travelled along the road, they came to a place where there was some water. The official had asked that since there was some water there, he would like to be baptized. Philip replied that he could, if he had believed with all his heart. The official said that he believed that Jesus was the Son of God. The official had asked his charioteer to stop. Then Philip and the official went down into the water, and Philip had baptized him. After they came out of the water, the Ethiopian official never saw Philip again. He was full of joy as he journeyed along. The Spirit of the Lord took Philip away. Philip later landed in Azotus. From there he traveled from town to town, all the way to Caesarea, speaking to the people he had come across about Lord Jesus. Philip later landed in Azotus. From there he traveled from town to town, on his way to Caesarea, speaking to the people he had come across about Lord Jesus.

ACTS 9

Saul the fanatic Jew of Tarsus in Cilicia on the east coast of the Mediterranean

- Saul becomes a follower of the Lord

The followers of the Lord at Jerusalem were under dire threat from the learned and bold fanatic Saul. Saul was determined to wipe out the new sect once and for all. He had even obtained from the Jerusalem high priest letters to the Yehudic leaders in Damascus in order to carry out his efforts at destroying the followers of Lord Jesus. He did this because he wanted to arrest and take to Jerusalem any man or woman who had become a follower of Lord Jesus. Saul, who had vowed to wipe out the followers of Lord Jesus, almost reached Damascus. Out of nowhere there flashed a bright light, which blinded Saul and he fell to the ground. Saul had heard a voice addressing him personally as to why he was so determined to persecute people Saul enquired as to who it was who had talked to him.

The answer had come instantly that it was it was Jesus, to whom Saul was so cruel. The voice had commanded that Saul should go into the city where he would be given further instructions. The men who had accompanied Saul became speechless. They could hear the speech but did

Acts 9

not see anybody around. Saul got up from the ground and when he had tried to open his eyes, he realized that he was blinded. Someone then gave him a hand and led him into Damascus. For three days Saul continued to grope around and could not see. He neither drank nor ate anything during his period of confusion.

There lived in Damascus Ananias, a follower of Lord Jesus. The Lord spoke to Ananias in a vision. Ananias responded that he was listening. Ananias was told to get up and visit the house of Judas, a leader among the fishermen on 'Straight Street.' Ananias would find a man named Saul from the city of Tarsus and that just then he was incessantly praying and fasting. Saul had seen a vision of a man named Ananias visiting him and placing his hands on him that he might regain his vision. (*Ananias could not believe what he heard*)

Ananias protested saying that a number of people had informed him about the awful things that Saul had been doing to the followers of Lord Jesus in Jerusalem. Now Saul had even obtained from the Jerusalem Yehudic hierarchy authorization to arrest anyone who was known to be a worshiper of Lord Jesus. The Lord had explained to Ananias that He had prepared Saul to be His envoy to foreigners, kings and the Jewish people. Lord Jesus was determined to use Saul greatly and that he would be persecuted for being a worshiper in the Lord's Name.

Ananias realized that it was a definite command from the Lord and that he had to obey the Lord's voice. Ananias got up and left to find the house where Saul was staying. Ananias placed his hands on Saul saying that Lord Jesus had sent him. He was the one who had stopped Saul on his way into Damascus. Lord Jesus would grant him his sight and in-fill him with the Holy Spirit.

As Ananias was talking, something like fish scales fell off Saul's eyes; and he regained his sight. Saul got up; and was baptized. Then he broke his fast and ate some food and drink and felt much better. Saul was encouraged to stay awhile among the Lord's followers at Damascus. (*He was instructed by the Lord's followers*).

- Saul preaches in Damascus

Saul was always enthusiastic in whatever he had done or said. Even though he was just new to the Faith in Lord Jesus, the Son of God, Saul entered the Yehudic meeting places and started propagating that Jesus was the Son of God. It was an astonishing claim since he had gone to Damascus to arrest the followers of Lord Jesus. People who heard Saul's propaganda in favour of the Lord were stunned and had wondered whether or not he was the man who came to arrest and drag them to the Jewish hierarchy at Jerusalem.

Saul had reasoned with great persuasive preaching with such power that the Yehudic leadership at Damascus were utterly confused. He had argued that Jesus was the Son of God; and for the Jewish people, Lord Jesus was their long awaited saviour.

Later, some of them made plans to kill Saul, but he had found out about it. He learned that they were guarding the gates of the city day and night in order to kill him. Then one night, his followers let him down over the city wall in a large basket.

- Saul in Jerusalem after conversion at Damascus

Saul later reached Jerusalem and wanted to join the Lord's followers. They were very worried about what to expect from the man who was out to get them in the first place. They were still leery of his intentions. Barnabas the elder and a big-hearted man took up the cause of Saul and introduced him to the Jerusalem followers of the Lord. He told them of Saul's experience on the road to Damascus and how he had witnessed powerfully and boldly in the name of Lord Jesus in Damascus.

Saul was then accepted by the Lord's followers and he freely witnessed to Lord Jesus in Jerusalem and told everyone about the Lord. Saul was an indefatigable debater, always arguing with the Yehudes who spoke Greek. They decided to put an end to Saul. The Lord's followers found out about this plot and sneaked Saul out to Caesarea. From there they shipped him off to his native city of Tarsus.

The church in Judaea, Galilee, and Samaria now enjoyed a time of peace; and worshiped the Lord. The small church community was strengthened, as the Holy Spirit encouraged it and helped it grow.

- Peter heals Aeneas

Peter, the chief apostle, travelled from place to place and visited the Lord's followers at Lydda. There he met a man named Aeneas, who was bed-ridden for eight years and could not even move (*perhaps paralysed*). Peter said to Aeneas that Lord Jesus had healed him and that Aeneas could get up and prepare something to eat. Right away he stood up. The people in the towns of Lydda and Sharon who knew about Aeneas and his recovery had become followers of the Lord.

- Peter brings Tabitha (*Dorcas*) back to Life

At Joppa lived Tabitha, a follower of the Lord, (*probably a Hellenist Yehude*) named Dorcas in Greek, which meant a deer. She was always doing good things for people and had given much to the poor. Tabitha got sick and died

[It was customary a dead person's body be washed and placed in an upstairs room for viewing and pre-burial arrangements.]

Joppa was close to Lydda where Peter was then residing. When the Lord's followers heard that Peter was at Lydda, they had sent two men to request Peter to come out to Joppa. They had urged Peter to get to Joppa right away. Peter got up and followed them.

When they reached the house of Tabitha they took Peter upstairs into the room where her body was laid. There was a lot of crying upstairs among the widowed who were helped in the past. They displayed to Peter all the clothing that Tabitha had made and given to them in the past. Peter persuaded everyone to leave the room and then knelt down and prayed. Then he turned towards the body and had ordered Tabitha to get up. The woman opened her eyes. When she saw Peter, she sat up. Peter took her by the hand and helped her to her feet.

Peter called in the widows and the other followers and presented Tabitha (*Dorcas*) who was resurrected. When the people of Joppa heard what had happened, many of them put their faith in the Lord. Peter had to stay on for a while in Joppa in the house of a man named Simon, who was a tanner. Peter helped the new followers in the ways of Lord Jesus

ACTS 10

Peter and Cornelius of the Imperial Guard – Jesus message was not of 'particularistic' but of 'universal' significance – Peter learned his lesson the hard way

- Peter and Captain Cornelius of the Roman garrison at Caesarea

Caesarea was a garrison city. Captain Cornelius was in-charge of the Italian Garrison. He was a devoutly religious person. He was probably either a convert to Judaism or, a genuine worshiper at the local Yehudic meeting place. His household were also worshipers. Cornelius was very liberal in his donations to the poor and he prayed regularly according to the Yehudic scheduled prayer times.

One afternoon, at the three o'clock prayer time Cornelius was present. He probably snoozed off and had a vision. He saw God's angel calling out to him by name. Cornelius was taken aback and stared at the angelic being. Then he queried as to what was the matter. The angel said that God had listened to his devotions and was aware of all his liberality towards the poor. He was told to send some men to Joppa to call on one named Simon Peter. They would find him residing with a tanner named Simon. The angel was gone.

Cornelius summoned two of his servants and one of his soldiers who also was a God-fearer. Cornelius told the three of what he had envisioned and sent them off to Joppa.

The delegation arrived in Joppa the next day about the noon hour. The house they were looking for had a flat roof with outside stairway to the roof top. At that very moment Peter was on the roof top for his afternoon devotions but he was very hungry. While the food was being prepared, Peter fell asleep and had a vision. In his visions Peter had seen that something was coming down, which looked like big canvas sailcloth held up at the four corners. Peter saw that the huge cloth contained all kinds of creatures – animals, birds, snakes and other creepy types. Peter heard a voice ordering Peter to get up, kill the creepy creatures and to eat them. In his dream, Peter protested claiming that he could not consume the creatures which were forbidden under his dietary traditions. As a Yehude, Peter had never eaten anything that was considered as 'unclean' therefore, unfit for human consumption. Peter heard the voice again saying that when God had said that something could be eaten he could not claim that it was not fit to eat because of his own dietary traditions.

Peter had experienced this vision three times during his snooze, before the sheet was suddenly withdrawn. While Peter was puzzled; and was wondering what the dreams meant, the three men from Cornelius had arrived at the gate of the house of Simon the Tanner. They were asking, if Simon Peter was residing there.

Peter was still puzzled over the vision, but the Holy Spirit goaded him that there were some men looking for him and that he had to go with them. He was not to worry about his self imposed dietary restrictions. The Lord had sent them. Peter the chief apostle did not hesitate any longer. He went down the outside stairs and met the men from Joppa. He invited the visitors in saying that he was the one they were looking for. Peter enquired as to what they wanted.

Acts 10

The men sent by Cornelius had explained that Captain Cornelius of the Caesarean garrison had sent them to Peter. They had persuasively argued that Cornelius was one of the devout Roman garrison commanders, who worshiped the God of the Yehudic people, a God-fearer. The Yehudic folks were approving of him and liked him well. One of the angels of the God of the Yehudes told Cornelius to send for Peter. He wishes to hear more about what Peter had to say. Peter invited them to spend the night.

Early next morning, Peter and a few other followers of the Lord at Joppa, had accompanied the three guests from Cornelius and they had left for Caesarea. Cornelius was waiting for them. He had also invited his kin and some of his close friends.

Cornelius greeted Peter upon his arrival and knelt at his feet and offered worship. Peter protested and taking hold of Cornelius requested him not to offer worship to him. Peter was just another human being like the rest of them.

Along with Cornelius, Peter entered into the house. There were many gathered in the house and they welcomed him. Peter cited a custom prevalent among the Yehudes not to get involved with non-Yehudes. It took him so long to realize that they were all equal before God and man. Peter had learned the hard way that there were no clean or unclean human beings. He indicated that the traditions among the Yehudes were very Jewish traditionalist. When the three men were knocking at the door of Simon the Tanner, Peter had responded and had agreed to travel with them immediately to Cornelius. He would have loved to know the reason why the Garrison commander had sent for him.

Cornelius had replied, four days ago at about three in the afternoon as a follower of Yehudic religious custom, he was offering prayers at home. Suddenly Cornelius had envisioned some personage who appeared in bright clothes and told him that God has heard his prayers and of his generosity to the poor. The personage had asked Cornelius to send someone to Joppa to fetch Simon Peter who was visiting with Simon the Tanner. He would guide him on how to proceed. Cornelius had therefore sent for Peter. The Garrison commander and his family were glad that Peter had accepted the request. All of them were in the presence of the Lord God, so that they could hear what Peter had to say.

The apostle Peter realized that his vision of the sheet of creepy creatures had great significance towards the universality of Lord Jesus Way. God had treated all people alike. God was pleased with everyone who worshiped him and did right, no matter what nation they came from. Peter went on to show that Lord Jesus was the one who gave peace to all who believed in him. He was himself anointed with the Spirit of God.

Elaborating further, Peter continued the story of Jesus, his rejection, crucifixion, death, resurrection, and his gift of the Holy Spirit to the apostles and many others assembled together at Jerusalem during the Yehudic Festival of Pentecost. They who were disciples of Lord Jesus and his apostles were to proclaim the good news of freedom from sin and damnation to a new life. All who had put their trust in Jesus and affirmed their faith by their willingness to be baptized in Jesus Name would gain eternal life.

Peter mentioned about the propagation of Jesus message by the apostles and the other followers who may not have seen him or ate and drank with him after he was raised from death. The close knit followers were the ones God had chosen to tell people of all nations about Jesus. Peter went on to assert that God had told them to inform everyone that Jesus was the one He has chosen to judge the living and the dead. All who had faith in him would have their sins forgiven in his Name.

Astonishingly, while Peter was still continuing with his message, the Holy Spirit took control of everyone who was intently listening to Peter's message. Some of the Yehudic followers of the Lord, who had accompanied Peter to Caesarea were surprised that the Holy Spirit had come upon the Gentiles as well. Those who came with Peter were hearing the Gentiles speaking in unknown languages and praising God.

The Gentiles were experiencing the gift of the Holy Spirit, just as the apostles and the other early Jewish followers of Lord Jesus were. Peter suggested that he was certain that no body should dare to stop him from baptizing Cornelius and his household. Peter arranged for Cornelius and all those assembled in his house to be baptized in the name of Lord Jesus. Cornelius had pleaded with Peter to stay with them for a few more days and enable them to learn more about the Lord and Peter had accepted their invitation.

[Baptism was by immersion and it was in the name of the Father, the Son and the Holy Spirit ever one God unto ages and ages. The Baptismal formulae as stated elsewhere had evolved over a few decades.]

ACTS 11

Peter's report of the new phenomenon of non-Jewish converts to the community of the 'Jesus Way' in Jerusalem and Caesarea

- Peter gave his reports to the Church in Jerusalem about Gentile conversions

The news about Gentiles becoming followers of Lord Jesus spread among the apostles resident in Jerusalem and among the Yehudic Christians in Judaea. When Peter came to Jerusalem, some of the Yehudic turned followers of the Lord insisted that the Gentile followers also had to follow the Yehudic old-time rituals including circumcision. They accused Peter of polluting himself by eating and staying in the homes of the Gentile turned followers of the Lord.

Peter had to defend himself by narrating the whole episodes including his dreams and the angelic guidance towards the conversion of the Roman Captain Cornelius and his family who were devout God-fearers at Caesarea. Peter also mentioned about how while he was preaching, the gift of the Holy Spirit came to the Gentiles. It happened in the same fashion as the apostolic community was in-filled with the Holy Spirit on the day of the Feast of Pentecost.

Peter had reasoned that he could not resist God's gifts to those Gentiles, which he and the apostolic community received themselves! How could he have dared to go against God?

Peter's persuasive speech convinced the challengers and they stopped arguing. Instead of grumbling any more they began praising God. They were glad that God had let Gentiles turn to him, and had given eternal life to them!

- The Church in Antioch

Since the murder of Stephen by stoning, some of the Lord's followers had been scattered all over Judaea, Samaria and as far as Phoenicia, Cyprus, and Antioch. These towns already had a Jewish population. The disciples, the Lord's followers, who were scattered in these locations spoke to the Yehudic communities and some of them became the followers of the Lord. They restricted their evangelism only to the Yehudic communities.

Some followers of Lord Jesus from Cyprus and Cyrene went to Antioch, an important city and started preaching to the Gentiles (*i.e., those Greek converts who were not of Jewish background*) the good news about Lord Jesus. It was marvellous that the power of the Lord was with them; and many of the Gentile citizenry put their faith in Jesus and became his followers. The news of what was taking place among the Gentiles spread to the church in Jerusalem.

The Jerusalem church decided to send the wise elder Barnabas to Antioch to strengthen them in their faith. Barnabas was amazed and glad at what God had done among the people of Antioch. He encouraged the Antiochean new followers to remain faithful with all their heart. The elder Barnabas was a man of great faith and was filled with the Holy Spirit. Many more people turned to the Lord through his ministry.

Barnabas left for Tarsus in search of Saul and found him and brought him to Antioch. Barnabas and Saul met with the church in Antioch for a whole year and instructed many of the converts in the ways of Lord Jesus. It was in Antioch that the Lord's followers were first called 'Christians.'

[In this redactor's view, a more cumbersome, but realistic descriptive concept should have been found and used. The concept of 'Christ' only reemphasized the Jewish ideology and quest for a powerful saviour who would overthrow the Roman yoke in politico-material terms. However, Lord Jesus was and is God's Son, incarnated *Yesu Avtar*. He was not a Jewish *Sage*. He was and is **the universal Lord and true Avtar**, among human communities]

During this great evangelistic awakening some preachers (*exhorters*) from Jerusalem came to Antioch. Agabus was one of them. Filled with the power of the Holy Spirit, Agabus predicted of the coming famine throughout the Empire, which happened when Claudius was Emperor (*AD41 – AD54*). Consequently, the followers of Lord Jesus in Antioch decided to send whatever help they could to the Lord's followers in Judaea who seemed to have many poor and were often poverty stricken. Barnabas and Saul took gifts from the Antiochean church to the church leaders in Jerusalem.

ACTS 12

Herod Antipas I the grand son of Herod the Great caused trouble for the church

Herod Antipas the grand son of Herod the Great was made the Roman procurator of Jerusalem. He caused much suffering for the followers of Lord Jesus. He ordered his guards to execute James the brother of John who was the leader among the Lord's followers at the Jerusalem church. When Herod realized that his action pleased the Jewish establishment, he decided to arrest Peter. It was the time of Passover festival (*festival of thin bread*) hence Peter was put in jail with a detail of forty soldiers to guard him. Herod had planned on putting Peter on a public trial after the festival. The followers of the Lord had prayed unceasingly to God on behalf of Peter.

- Peter was rescued

On the day prior to the public trial, four soldiers were on guard – two on either side of the chained Peter in the jail-cell; and two at the entrance to the jail. An angel from the Lord appeared and light flooded the cell. The angel woke Peter and ordered him to get up, get dressed and lash up his sandals. Peter in a daze did what he was told. The chains fell off from his hands and ankles. He was further instructed to put on his outerwear and coat and to follow the angel. Peter just followed and thought it was all a dream. They went past the soldiers; and when they came to the iron jail-gate it opened by itself! They went out; and as they were walking along the street, the angel was gone and Peter was all alone. It was then that Peter became fully aware of what was occurring. He said to himself that it must have been the Lord who sent his angel to rescue him from Herod and the Yehudic leaders.

Then Peter headed to the house of Mary the mother of John Mark where the Lord's followers were holed up in intense prayer. Peter knocked at the outer gate, and Rhoda a maid came to answer. On hearing Peter's voice yelling to let him in, Rhoda was too excited to open the gate but ran up-stairs to let the company know that Peter was standing outside the gate.

Everyone assembled in the room told her that she must have been crazy. Rhoda had insisted that it was Peter. Then they pacified Rhoda by consoling her that it must have been Peter's guardian angel. Peter continued knocking. Finally someone came out and opened the gate.

When the disciples saw Peter they were utterly amazed. Peter motioned for silence and explained what had happened. He asked the group to let James, the brother of the Lord and the others know what has happened. Peter immediately left the place and hid somewhere else.

When the morning came, the soldiers on guard were terribly confused, worried and wondered what could have happened to Peter. Herod Antipas ordered his own soldiers to search for Peter, but they could not find him either. Then Herod was furiously questioning the guards and not satisfied with their responses, put them to death. After this, Herod left Judaea to stay in Caesarea for a while.

[This story resonates with some of the modern day justice for the defenceless! The liberation of the poor in

Tunisia, Egypt, Libya and especially the poorest of the poor, outcaste-ridden societies come to mind]

- Herod Antipas I dies

Herod's taxation policies were irksome for the people of the port cities of Tyre and Sidon. They were very angry. Unfortunately for the citizens of Tyre and Sidon, they were dependent for their food supply on the region where Herod Antipas ruled. A delegation from the two cities went to see Blastus, one of the high officials of the King's bureaucracy. They convinced Blastus that they would submit to some terms with the King. A day was set for them to meet with Herod Antipas.

Herod came out in his royal regalia. Seated on his throne, Herod Antipas made a powerful oration. The people were overawed. They exclaimed that Antipas spoke more like a god than a human. Herod was quite pleased with himself. Alas! This act of self adulation displeased God as Herod failed to acknowledge God but gloried in himself. An angel from the Lord struck him down. Herod Antipas died, probably of stomach ulcers. Lord Jesus message spread far and wide.

Heretofore, we will hear the story of the newly emergent leader Saul under the wings of Barnabas. After Barnabas and Saul had completed their evangelistic work, accompanied by John Mark they went back to Antioch. However, John Mark's home was in Jerusalem.

ACTS 13

Barnabas and Saul sent out with the blessings of the Syrian Antioch Church

- Barnabas and Saul were chosen and sent

There were many spiritual leaders and teachers in the Antiochean Church. Some of them were Barnabas, Simeon, who was also known as Niger, Lucius from Cyrene, Manaen a close friend of Herod Antipas and Saul. During their worship of the Lord and fasting, the Holy Spirit instructed them to appoint Barnabas and Saul to carry out the work, for which the Lord had chosen them. Hearing this call, everyone prayed and fasted for a while longer. Afterwards, the leaders and the congregation appointed Barnabas and Saul for the special mission by the laying on of their hands. Then everyone with one accord sent them away.

- Barnabas and Saul in Cyprus

Barnabas and Saul sent by the Holy Spirit went down to Seleucia, the port town. There they boarded a ship which was bound for the island of Cyprus. When they arrived at Salamis on the east coast, Barnabas and Saul started their preaching work in the Yehudic meeting places. John Mark was with them as a helper. The preaching tour took Barnabas and Saul all the way to the city of Paphos on the west end of the island. There the apostles met a Yehude by the name of Bar-Jesus, (*also known as Elymas*) who had practiced witchcraft. Bar Jesus was in cahoots with the governor of the island, Sergius Paulus. The governor was a very smart man. He wanted to hear what Barnabas and Saul had to say about God. But Elymas was opposed to the idea of the governor listening to Barnabas and Saul, the travelling evangelists. He tried to keep the governor from putting his faith in Lord Jesus.

The no nonsense Saul, being filled with the Holy Spirit looked straight at Elymas and rebuked that Elymas was a son of the evil one and that he was a liar, a crook, and an enemy of everything that was right. Saul enquired whether Elymas would ever stop speaking against the true ways of the Lord. The Lord would punish him for a while and that he would go blind.

Immediately, Elymas' eyes developed a dark mist; and he groped around trying to get someone to lead him by the hand. When Sergius Paulus, the governor saw what was going on, he was impressed and put his faith in Lord Jesus after he heard Barnabas and Saul.

- Barnabas and Saul in Antioch of Pisidia

From Paphos they caught the ship sailing to Perga in Pamphylia. John Mark had left them at Paphos and returned to his home in Jerusalem. Barnabas, Saul and the rest of them went on from Perga to Antioch in Pisidia. In all these cities there were Yehudic settlements. Since they were waiting for a ship, on the next Yehudic day of worship (*Friday evening till Saturday evening*) they attended worship at the Yehudic meeting place. After the reading of the Yehudic scriptures the leaders sent someone over to ask Barnabas and Saul if they had anything to say that would help the people, to exhort them. Saul was ready to proclaim the good news! He motioned with his hand and gave a history lesson on the Yehudic people and their sojourn over the centuries.

Then he hastened to speak about the Lord. Jesus, the Son of God, had become human and went about doing good, healing the physically and mentally challenged and even raisiting people from death. But the Yehudic people of Jerusalem, Judaea and Samaria were looking for someone who could overthrow the Roman yoke and enable them to acquire independence and prosperity. Jesus did not fit the bill. So, they had him put to death. But God raised him from death and his body did not decay! Then for many days Jesus appeared to his followers who had gone with him from Galilee to Jerusalem. They were reaching out to the Yehudic Diaspora. Saul challenged those present at worship in the meeting place saying that Jesus would forgive their sins and grant them eternal life.

As Barnabas and Saul were about to leave the meeting, the people begged them to say more about those same things at the next worship. After the service, many Yehudes and a lot of Gentile god-fearers went with them. Barnabas and Saul urged them all to remain faithful to God, who had been very kind to them.

At the next Yehudic worship almost everyone in town came to hear about the Lord. When the suspicious Yehudic leaders saw the crowds, they became very jealous. They insulted Saul and spoke against everything he had said. Barnabas and Saul boldly asserted that they had to tell God's message to those Yehudes first, before they proclaimed it to others. They seemed to reject it! Perhaps they did not deserve eternal life. The evangelists would go to the Gentiles.

The Gentiles were glad to hear what Barnabas and Saul had to say. Many of them who heard about the Lord put their faith in Him. The good news of Lord Jesus spread all over that region! The jealous Yehudic leaders got in touch with some of their friends among the important folks of the town and incited them to turn against Barnabas and Saul. They even persuaded some of the respected devout women. They turned them against Barnabas and Saul and started making trouble for them. The Jewish leaders managed to get Barnabas and Saul chased-out of that part of the country.

Barnabas and Saul went on to the city of Iconium. The Lord's followers in Antioch in Pisidia were very glad for the Lord's message and were filled with the Holy Spirit.

ACTS 14

Barnabas and Saul in Iconium and Lystra in the Province of Galatia

- Barnabas and Saul on evangelistic trip in Iconium

The missionary strategy of Barnabas and Saul was to gain converts from the Yehudic communities spread abroad in the Roman Empire, particularly in the Greek cities in the Mediterranean. They would join worship at the Yehudic meeting places and then speak to them about Jesus as their expected saviour and urge them to put their trust in Lord Jesus.

Barnabas and Saul entered the Yehudic meeting place in Iconium in the province of Galatia, just as they did at Antioch in Pisidia. Many Yehudes and the Gentile god-fearers who were at worship in the meeting place put their faith in the Lord. But the Yehudes who would not be persuaded by the two evangelists, stirred up the other Gentile god-fearers to anger against the Lord's followers. However, Barnabas and Saul weathered the storm and stayed on at Iconium for a while trusting in the Lord's protection. They continued to speak bravely in the Lord's Name. They were once again enabled by the Lord to work miracles and wonders. These actions confirmed to the people of God's great kindness.

The people of Iconium did not know what to think! Some of them sided with the Yehudic detractors, while others trusted the apostles. The matter became so serious that some Greeks and Yehudes, together with their leaders, decided to make trouble for Barnabas and Saul and to stone them to death. The two apostles learned about the brewing antagonism, decided to leave town. They preached the good news in the towns of Lystra and Derbe and in the nearby countryside.

- Barnabas and Saul evangelize in Lystra

At Lystra there was a born lame man who attended the gatherings at which Barnabas and Saul were speaking. Saul realized that the crippled man had faith in Lord Jesus and was ripe for healing. Fixing his gaze intently on the lame man, Saul shouted at him to stand up. Immediately the lame man jumped up and began to walk.

When the crowd saw what happened, they yelled out in the dialect of Lycaonia claiming that the gods had come down to them in human form. They called Barnabas Zeus, and Saul became Hermes (*Hermes was the divine messenger of other gods to Zeus the chief Greek God*) because Saul did the talking.

The temple of Zeus was close to the city-gate. The priest and the crowds immediately wanted to offer a sacrifice to Barnabas and Saul. The priest rushed out to get some bulls and flowers. When the two apostles realized what was occurring, they tore their outer wear in horror and ran into the gathered devotees and shouted that they were ordinary humans like the people of Lystra. They should not do anything foolhardy; instead they had to turn to the living God there and then!

Barnabas and Saul could not stop the people from offering a sacrifice to them. However, some of the Yehudic leaders from Antioch and Iconium got wind of what was taking place. They came over and managed to turn the crowds against Saul the healer of the lame man. They stoned Saul and dragged him out of the city, thinking he was dead. When the furor died down, some of the Lord's followers came out of the city wall and gathered around Saul in great sorrow. When Saul regained consciousness and saw the presence of the Lord's followers, he stood up. Saul and Barnabas went back with those followers of Lord Jesus into the city. The next morning the Lord's followers managed to get them out of the city. Barnabas and Saul landed in Derbe.

- Barnabas and Saul return to Antioch in Syria after their mission trip

Barnabas and Saul spread the good news in Derbe; and some of those who listened put their faith in Lord Jesus. Then they journeyed back to Lystra, Iconium, and Antioch in Pisidia encouraging the Lord's followers in those areas, urging them to remain faithful. The apostles spoke of the sufferings the Lord's followers may have to endure on earth.

Barnabas and Saul recommended to the newly formed Christian communities some names for leadership roles. Then they fasted and prayed that the Lord would take good care of those leaders. Barnabas and Saul went on through Pisidia to Pamphylia, where they preached in the city of Perga (*probably at the Yehudic meeting place, which was the pattern of evangelistic endeavours of all the apostles and their disciple-leaders*). Then they caught a ship at Attalia (the nearest seaport) which was headed to Antioch in Syria from where they were commissioned for their missionary activities which were completed.

After arriving in Antioch, they met with the apostles, church leaders and the congregation. They gave a report on their mission activities among the Yehudic communities. They also provided a report on how God had guided them to reach out to the Gentiles (i.e., Greeks, some of whom were god-fearers) to become followers of the Lord. At Antioch in Syria the two apostles stayed put with the followers of the Lord for a long time.

ACTS 15

Jerusalem Jewish Church leaders meet to decide on acceptance of Gentile converts *on par* and gave letters to the evangelists – Saul goes his own way

- Insistence of Jewish Christians on imposing their ritual practices on Gentile converts

The Yehudic Christians kept insisting on the Gentile converts following the Yehudic ritualistic practices if they were to attain salvation and eternal life. Some of these Yehudic Christians came out from Judaea and started teaching the Lord's followers that they could not be saved, unless they were circumcised according to their ancient Yehudic laws.

[Here was a classic example of the Yehudes and the Yehudic-Christians not grasping the new phenomenon that with the Incarnate Lord Jesus, the Yehudic laws were of no consequence as faith in Jesus as Son of God was the only basis for eternal life. The behavioural norms of the society in which one lived were the *modus operandi*. The time frame of the Graeco-Roman world applied to all people irrespective of their Faith in Lord Jesus or, any other Faith system. Furthermore, some scholars have held that in the earliest times of the spread of Christianity in the Roman Empire, some of the Yehudes became jealous of the success rate of conversion to Jesus Way, that they deliberately identified themselves as Christian only in name to provide them an opportunity to throw a wrench into the phenomenal inroads the apostles were making among the Gentiles]

The intervention by the Yehudic Christians in the lives of the Gentile converts to Lord Jesus way caused confusion and anxiety among the Gentile converts. Barnabas and Saul tried to persuade the Yehudic Christians that they could not impose Yehudic rituals on the non-Yehudic (*or, on non-practicing Jews for that matter*) new followers of Lord Jesus. Some of the fanatic Yehudic Christians would not yield ground. Reluctantly, the Antiochean Christian community decided to send Barnabas, Saul and a few others to Jerusalem to discuss the issue and get a ruling from the apostles and the Jerusalem/Judaean church leaders.

- Church leaders meet in Jerusalem over Yehudic-ritual and sexuality issues

The delegates journeyed to Jerusalem, via Phoenicia and Samaria, and preached to people as they travelled about the Gentiles accepting the Lord. The news of Gentile conversions made the Lord's followers (*who were primarily of Yehudic background*) very happy. When the delegates arrived in Jerusalem, they were warmly welcomed by the primarily Jewish-Christian community and the apostolic leadership.

The delegates briefed the Jerusalem Christians about everything God had done. Some of the Pharisees turned followers of the Lord stood up and insisted that the Gentiles who had become the Lord's followers had to submit to circumcision. They also had to be told to obey the Yehudic ancient Laws. In other words, they saw the Jesus movement as no more than a Yehudic reform movement.

[Here is the crux of the issue which has afflicted Christians for two thousand years. Incarnation was sidestepped in favour of following Jewish historical traditions and behavioural norms. The concept of incarnation while prevalent in Hinduism and Buddhism was alien to the Jewish community.]

The Church leaders including the apostles wrestled with the issue of Gentile converts for a long time and were exhausted. Finally, Peter got up and announced that they were well aware that long ago God let him be the one from their group to preach the good news to the Gentles.

God had decided it, so that the Gentiles would also hear the good news and become followers of the Lord along side of the Yehudic converts to the Lord's Way. God knew what was in everyone's heart. He had clearly and in no uncertain way showed to the apostolic team that He had equally chosen the Gentiles, when he gave them the gift of the Holy Spirit, just as he had given his Spirit to the Hellenists and Judaean Yehudic-converts to Jesus Way. They put their faith in Lord Jesus, and he made their hearts pure.

[Peter was referring to Captain Cornelius and many of the Gentile god-fearers becoming Christians under his ministry]

Peter pressed on, questioning as to why the Yehude-turned Christians were trying to make God angry by placing a heavy burden on the new Gentile followers. This burden of the Yehudic Ritualistic requirement was too heavy for the apostles and to their ancestors. Lord Jesus was kind to the apostolic community. They were saved now by faith in Him alone, just as the new Gentile-converts had faith in him alone. Barnabas and Saul told their stories of how God had given them the power to work a lot of miracles and wonders for the Gentiles. After the lengthy debates, James, the Lord's brother had urged the people to listen to him. Simon Peter had just then informed of how God first came to the Gentiles and made some of them His own people.

So! Let them not add any more Yehudic burdens on the Gentiles who were turning to God. Let the apostles simply send them a note urging the Gentile converts to avoid idolatry and eating things ritually offered to idols; and the meat of the strangled creatures the blood of which was still intact. The new converts must also be asked not to commit any sexual immorality, either fornication or adultery.

[This minimal constraint may refer to the ancient ways of ensuring the birth of a son to carry forward the lineage by marrying next in line brother in the Patriarchal system. Perhaps, Saul was also referring to plain sexual immorality of the times.]

- Jerusalem leaders' letter to Gentiles who became followers of Lord Jesus

Having made the decision on Gentile convert requirements, the apostles, the leaders, and all the church members in Jerusalem decided to send some men to Antioch along with Barnabas and Saul. They chose Silas and Judas Barsabbas (*who may have been a brother of Joseph Barsabbas, the step-father of our Lord*) who were two leaders of the Lord's followers. They also wrote a letter that said that the apostles and leaders were sending friendly greetings to all of the Gentiles turned followers of the Lord in Antioch, Syria, and Cilicia.

The apostolic community acknowledged its disappointment with the fanatical behavioural requirements of the Yehude turned Christians of Jerusalem and Judaea. The apostles did not send any instructions regarding the Hellenistic converts' behavioural norms. Since some outside elements created a fuss, they met together and decided to choose some men and to send them to Jerusalem along with the good friends Barnabas and Saul. These men had risked their lives for Lord Jesus. They were also pleased to let

Judas and Silas visit with the Gentile converts and explain in person the same things that were also put in writing.

This much was clear. The Holy Spirit had shown them that they should not place any extra burden on the Gentile converts. The only common sense suggestions to the Gentile converts were that they refrain from idolatry and sexual temple prostitutions. If they adhered to such broad based moral requirements, they will do well. They concluded with their best wishes!

When the four men arrived in Antioch, they got in touch with the Antiochean church leadership and the church members together and presented the letter from the Jerusalem Church. Upon the Jerusalem note being read in public everyone was pleased and greatly encouraged. Judas and Silas having oratory gift, spoke powerfully for a long time, encouraging and helping the Lord's followers.

The deputation from Jerusalem found favour with the Antiochean church; and they stayed on in Antioch of Syria for a while. And when they had finally left to return to Jerusalem, the Lord's followers in Antioch of Syria were grateful and wished them farewell. But Barnabas and Saul (*and possibly Silas too*) stayed on in Antioch, which was fast becoming the centre of Gentile Christianity where they and many others taught and preached about the Lord. While the Yehudic Christianity was centred in Jerusalem and Judaea, the Gentile Christendom was Antioch based.

- Barnabas and Saul go their separate ways

Saul suggested to Barnabas that they might re-visit the Lord's followers in the cities where they had preached the Lord's message. Then they would know how well they were doing. Barnabas agreed to Saul's suggestion and wished to invite John Mark along. Saul didn't like the idea, because John Mark had not continued with them at Pamphylia and had returned to his home in Jerusalem. With his sense of commitment to the preaching of the Gospel Saul felt reluctant to invite John Mark, who had left the team in the middle of a mission trip to attend to his own business interests at Jerusalem. However, John Mark and his mother provided much support for the Lord's followers at Jerusalem.

Saul and Barnabas argued over John Mark's accompanying them. This argument led to Saul and Barnabas going their separate ways. Barnabas accompanied by John Mark boarded a ship that sailed to Cyprus. After the blessings of the followers of the Lord, taking Silas with him, Saul left on a tour of encouragement of the converts in the cities and countryside where Barnabas and he had helped establish Christian communities in the provinces of Syria and Cilicia.

ACTS 16

Saul heads his own team with Silas and Timothy

- Timothy joined team Saul and Silas

Saul and Silas visited Derbe and Lystra, where there was a follower named Timothy. His mother was also a follower. She was Yehudic, but Timothy's father was a Greek. The Lord's followers in Lystra and Iconium spoke highly of Timothy. Saul wanted Timothy to accompany them in their missionary venture. Saul had him first circumcised, because all the Jewish people around there knew that Timothy's father was Greek.

[Saul had felt that it would have been strategically useful to have Timothy circumcised to present him as a genuine follower of the Yehudic ways in spite of the fact that Timothy's father was a known Greek. Was this move a blessing?]

As Saul and the others went from city to city, they told the Lord's followers about the Jerusalem decision on issues of circumcision and other Yehudic rituals. The Lord's followers were not to be required to conform to the Yehudic practices. The churches became stronger in their faith in Lord Jesus; and each day more people put their faith in the Lord.

- Saul's vision in Troas

Saul and his friends passed through Phrygia and Galatia to encourage the Lord's followers; and to further evangelize. However, the Holy Spirit would not permit them to do further evangelistic work in the area known as 'Asia.' After Saul and his team got to Mysia, they tried to get into Bithynia, but the Spirit of Jesus denied them access. They ended up in Troas. Saul had a vision during the night, in which someone from Macedonia was urging him to go there and help out. Saul was now eager to get into Macedonia. He was looking for a passage on board any ship headed that way. Saul and his companions felt sure that God had called them to preach the good news in Macedonia. They finally found a ship headed to Philippi. They booked passage and arrived at Samothrace, thence to Neopolis and arrived at Philippi, an important Roman colony in the first district of Macedonia.

- Lydia a rich clothes merchant becomes a follower of Lord Jesus

The team spent several days in Philippi. Saul used his old strategy of trying to join worship at a Yehudic meeting place. On the next Yehudic day of worship, Saul decided to check-out if there were any Yehudic meeting places for prayer, outside the city gate by the riverside.

Sure enough, Saul and team met a few women who were at a location close to the river. Saul went over and sat down with the women who were devout Yehudes, who had come out of the city for prayers.

One of the women was Lydia from the city of Thyatira who was a business-woman trading in expensive purple cloth. Lydia was a devout Yehudic worshiper of God. Saul persuaded her to become a follower of Lord Jesus. In a short while, Lydia and her family were ready for baptism.

After she and her family were baptized, she repeatedly urged Saul that if he had considered that Lydia truly had faith in the Lord, then he should consider staying at Lydia's house while the team was at Philippi. After some hesitation Saul and his team accepted Lydia's invitation.

- Saul and Silas were jailed

On one occasion, when Saul and team were on their way to the meeting place for prayer, they were met by a slave girl. She could forecast the future. Her abilities brought good income to her owners. The girl followed Saul and team and kept yelling that Saul and his companions were servants of the Most High God! They were telling the people how to attain eternal life.

The slave-girl kept on following the evangelists for several days. Finally, Saul couldn't take it any more; and turned around and rebuked the spirit, which possessed the girl that in the name of Lord Jesus to leave the girl alone! Immediately the evil spirit left the girl.

When the owners of the slave-girl realized that their chances to make money were gone, they grabbed hold of Saul and Silas and dragged them into the court. They complained against Saul and his team that they were upsetting the citizenry! They also claimed that Saul and company were demanding of the citizenry to do things they were not supposed to do.

[It was most likely that Saul was proclaiming Lord Jesus alone could be worshiped; and that the customary offering of a pinch of incense to the Emperor would be idolatrous]

Being goaded, the crowd joined in the attack on Paul and Silas. The city officials tore the outer-wear of Saul and Silas and ordered them to be whipped. After they were severely whipped and beaten they were ordered to be kept in jail and guarded extra carefully. The jailer did exactly as he was

Acts 16

told. He put Saul and Silas in the high security section and chained them to very heavy wooden blocks.

That night, the earth-quake struck about midnight as Saul and Silas were praying and singing praises to God. The other prisoners were curious about what was going on and listened to the two new inmates singing away. The strong earthquake shook the jail to its foundations. The doors flew wide open; and the chains fell off all the prisoners. Fortunately nobody escaped.

After all the commotion, the jailor went over to inspect for any possible damage. He was shocked to find all the jail cells were wide open. He assumed that the prisoners must have escaped and decided to kill himself with his sword. Saul foreseeing the situation shouted out to the jailor not to do himself any harm. No one had escaped. It was a relief. The jailor got a torch and entered the jail to check things out for his satisfaction and relief. He was shaking from head to foot. He did obeisance in front of Saul and Silas and led them out of their jail-cell and took them to his home and washed their wounds and begged the two as to what must he do to attain eternal life. They had replied asking the jailor to have faith in Lord Jesus and he and his household would experience peace and solace!

Saul and Silas witnessed to everyone else of the jailor's household about the Lord. While it was still night, the jailor took them to a place (*probably an ancient healthcare facility*) where he could attend to their cuts and bruises. After all the terrible lynching, etc., the jailor and his household were baptized; and became followers of Lord Jesus! They were exceedingly glad that they put their faith and trust in Lord Jesus! After all the panic settled down, the jailor took Saul and Silas to his own home and attended to their hunger needs. The next morning the Roman colonial bureaucrats of Philippi sent some police with orders for the jailer to let Paul and Silas go. The jailor was ever so glad to hear the order from the higher-ups. He told Saul that the colonial officials had ordered him to set Saul and Silas free; and they could leave in peace.

Saul was not going to quietly disappear. He told the police that they were Roman citizens, and the Roman colonial bureaucrats had them publicly whipped and beaten with sticks without following due process. To add to insult they even threw them into jail. And then, they had wished to get rid of them secretly. No, they could not do that. The city officials themselves had to come and let them out.

When the police told the bureaucrats that Saul and Silas were Roman citizens, the officials were scared. They came in a hurry and apologized and led them out of the jail and pleaded with them to leave town. But Saul and Silas went straight back to the home of Lydia, where they saw the Lord's followers and encouraged them. Then they packed-up and left town.

[Of the vast and far-flung Roman Empire, only a small percentage of the people were considered citizens. The citizen had special rights and privileges. The rest of the multitude, perhaps approximately 60 million were 'conquered' people, as such were not considered as citizens, but technically were **'slaves.'** In this regard, Alexander the Great, a Macedonian young general four centuries earlier was a much wiser man than the later Roman Generals. Alas! Alexander's own Generals were interested in gaining personal wealth and the Alexandrian Empire did not last long.]

ACTS 17

Saul and team reach out in Thessalonica, Berea in Macedonia and at Athens

- Trouble started brewing in Thessalonica

From Philippi, Saul, Silas and the team passed through (*no doubt, proclaiming the message of the Lord Jesus en route*) Amphipolis and Apollonia in Macedonia to Thessalonica, where there was a Yehudic settlement with its meeting place. Saul and team attended the Yehudic worship; and on three consecutive occasions Saul addressed the assembled Hellenistic Yehudes and their friends. Saul and Silas spoke of Lord Jesus as the Son of God, persecuted, put to death but rising again.

Some of the listeners believed what Saul had to say and they became followers of the Lord and joined hands with Saul and Silas. Some Gentiles (*usually refers to Greek converts to Yehudic religion*) and many important women also believed the message.

The Yehudic leaders, who watched the sway that Saul and team had, became jealous. It was also possible that the jealous group got some of the jobless ruffians who were hanging around the market-square to start a riot in the city. They wanted to drag Saul and Silas out to the mob, hence they ended-up straight to the house of Jason, a devout follower of the Lord.

When they did not find Saul or Silas at Jason's place, they were furious; and dragged out Jason and some of the Lord's followers whom they could find. They took them to the city authorities and accused Saul and Silas of upsetting Roman citizenry everywhere. Now they had come to Thessalonica and Jason had welcomed them into his home. All of them broke the laws of the Roman Emperor by claiming that someone named Jesus was king.

The city-officials and the citizenry were upset when they heard this. They forced Jason and the other known followers of the Lord to place bail-bonds to humiliate them and to scare other would be followers of Lord Jesus. Then the officials let Jason and the others go.

- People in Berea welcome the message about Lord Jesus

The Lord's followers decided to send Saul, Silas and Timothy to Berea in the interior not far from Thessalonica. After Saul and Silas got to Berea they joined the Yehudic meeting place for worship. The folks at Berea were very civil and gladly received the evangelists' preaching. The folks seriously examined the Yehudic scriptures to see if what the evangelists were claiming fitted their own perceptions. Many of them put their faith in the Lord. Some of them were important Greek women and several men also joined the Lord's followers.

The fanatical Yehudic leaders of Thessalonica had learned that Saul was in Berea preaching about Lord Jesus Way. So, they went to Berea and started stirring up the crowd against the evangelists.

Since Saul always was stirring-up the crowd through his vigorous orations, the Lord's followers sent him off to the Aegean coast as far as Athens, while Silas and Timothy stayed in Berea to help with instructing the new converts. Saul sent a message for Silas and Timothy to join him as soon as possible.

- Saul at Athens

Saul could not bear to see all the idolatry being practiced at Athens while he was waiting in Athens. As usual, Saul decided to visit the Yehudic meeting place and started speaking to those who worshipped there about Lord Jesus. Every day Saul was at the market-place proclaiming Jesus and engaging in conversation with anyone he met in the market. Some of them were Epicureans while some others were Stoics. Being philosophers they had decided to engage Saul in arguments. People were enquiring as to what the 'know-it-all' was trying to say.

[The Epicureans followed the philosophy of Epicurus who had taught that happiness should be the goal in life. The Stoics were the followers of the philosopher Zeno, who had taught that people should learn self-control and be guided by their conscience]

Some thought that Saul had been preaching about some foreign gods! That's what it must have meant, when Saul talked about Jesus and about people rising from death.

[This may refer to a Greek goddess named 'Rising from death.']

The philosophers brought Saul before an Areopagus (council), and had asked Saul to tell them more about his new teaching! They had heard Saul articulating some strange ideas, and they would love to know more about them.

Athenians and the foreigners living there were notorious for their desire to hear and argue about any thing new. Saul thinking it was an opportune moment got-up and stood in front of the council and said that the Athenians were very tolerant and permitted edifices for many Faiths. They had an altar with the words, "To an Unknown God." They permitted worship of the unknown God without knowing anything about Him. Saul had wished to say some thing about Him. Saul continued that their unknown God had created the world and everything in it. He was the God of all the heavens and the earth, who did not need any temples. He had provided life, breath, and everything else to all people. All human beings longed for him and were constantly trying to reach out and find him as all human beings were his children, just as some of the Greek poets had affirmed. Saul maintained that God was challenging them to turn to Him. He had chosen a man Jesus, who Saul had believed was the Son of God, incarnate in human flesh. God wanted people to believe on Him for their own wellbeing. Jesus was put to death at the instigation of the Yehudic people of Judaea. But God raised him to life. Saul had urged them to have faith in him.

Some of the people laughed when they heard Saul claimed that Jesus was raised from death. Others had said that they would listen to Saul's claims on another day. When Saul left the council meeting, some of the men who listened put their faith in the Lord and went with Saul. One of them was a council member, named Dionysius. There was also a woman Damaris and many others also put their faith in Lord Jesus.

ACTS 18

Saul and team visit Corinth and re-visit other places strengthening believers there

- Saul at Corinth

Saul decided to leave Athens and visit Corinth which was also an important commercial city. There he gained the acquaintance of Aquila, a prominent Jew from Pontus. Before this, Aquila and his wife Priscilla had come out of Italy, because of Emperor Claudius expulsion of the Yehudic settlers from Rome. (*It is possible that the expulsion occurred in AD 49 or, perhaps in AD 41*).

Saul found out that Aquila and Priscilla were tent makers as he himself was. So he stayed with them, and they worked together. Saul joined the Yehudic worship at their meeting place. As was his strategy, he engaged the Yehudes, the Hellenists and other Greeks and tried to win them over to Lord Jesus Way.

After Silas and Timothy rejoined him from Macedonia, he spent all his time preaching to the Yehudes about Jesus as their long awaited *Sage*. After a while, the targeted community could no longer tolerate Saul and started insulting him. So, Saul shook the dust from his clothes (*It was the same ideology of rejection as shaking off the dust from the feet*).

Saul even dared to berate them that whatever befell them, it would have been due to their rejection of the message about Lord Jesus Way. He would be blameless since he had tried to proclaim Lord Jesus as their long awaited *Sage*. Saul went further (*as if he was drawing the line in the sand*) saying, that from then on he would preach to the Gentiles.

Then Saul took up residence in the house of Titus Justus, a Yehudic proselyte, who followed the Yehudic worship. Titus Justus lived next door to the Yehudic meeting place. The leader of the Yehudic meeting place was Crispus. He and all the members of his family put their faith in the Lord. Many more Corinthians, who learned about Lord Jesus, put their faith in Him and were baptized.

On one occasion Saul had one of his visions, in which the Lord had encouraged him not to be afraid to preach about faith in Lord Jesus. Saul should not stop preaching. Lord Jesus was with him, and no harm would come to him. There were many in Corinth who would respond to his call to faith in Lord Jesus. Saul stayed on in Corinth for a year and a half, teaching the Lord's ways to the people.

During the governorship of Gallio of the province of Achaia, some of the frustrated, jealous and angry Yehudic leaders grabbed Saul and brought him into court, and accused Saul saying that he was antagonizing them by trying to persuade their people that their Laws and worship were insufficient and that they had to turn to Jesus of Nazareth, who was put to death a few years earlier on.

Saul was about to defend himself. But Governor Gallio said that if they were charging the man with a crime or some other wrong, he would have to listen to them. Since the accusations they were making concerned only words, names, and their own ancient traditions, they had better take care of them themselves. Gallio would not make any judgement over such matters. Then Gallio sent them out of the court. The angry crowd grabbed Sosthenes, the Yehudic leader, and beat him up in front of the court. But Gallio paid no attention to this act of defiant instigation.

- Saul returns to Antioch in Syria

Saul stayed on and worked with the Corinthian church for some more time and said good-bye and sailed on to Syria with Aquila and Priscilla. Before he left, he had his head shaved at Cenchreae because he had made a promise to God.

[Saul had earlier on in life promised to be a 'Nazarite!' This meant that for the time of the promise he could not cut his hair or drink wine. When the avowed period was completed, he could cut his hair and offer a sacrifice to God. Was it possible that Saul got bored easily and became restless? Obviously he was a man of action and preferred to be engaged.]

The three of them arrived in Ephesus, where Saul had left Priscilla and Aquila. Saul then entered the Yehudic meeting place to speak of Lord Jesus. The Lord's followers at Ephesus urged Saul to stay on for a longer visit, but Saul refused. Once again, it was time for Saul to say his good-byes! He said that if God lets him, he could come back.

Saul boarded a ship sailing to Caesarea. Upon arrival, he met with the congregation and exchanged greeting and words of encouragement. Then he was on his way to Antioch (*in Phrygia?*). After staying there for a while, Saul moved on and visited several towns and cities in Galatia and Phrygia. He provided counselling to many of the followers towards strengthening their faith in Lord Jesus.

- Apollos in Ephesus

There was a devout Yehude Apollos who visited Ephesus. Apollos was an Alexandrian by birth and was a good orator. He knew a lot about the Yehudic Scriptures. Apollos was also well aware about the Lord's Way (*i.e., the life-styles of the Lord's followers*). He spoke about it with great enthusiasm. Whatever he taught about Jesus were valid, however his knowledge was rather limited. All he knew was John's message about baptism. Apollos addressed the Yehudic community boldly in their meeting place. But when Priscilla and Aquila heard him, they took him to their home and helped him understand Lord Jesus Way even better.

Apollos being an enthusiast had decided to visit the Lord's followers in all of Achaia. So the Lord's followers wrote letters of commendation, to the followers of Jesus Way in all Achaia to welcome him. When he arrived in Achaia, he received a welcome support and help from everyone who had faith in Lord Jesus because of God's kindness. He got into fierce debates with the Yehudic leadership in public. He quoted the Yehudic sacred text to show that Jesus was the long awaited *Sage*.

ACTS 19

Saul gets into trouble at Ephesus over many icons prevalent there

- Saul at Ephesus

Apollos stayed on in Corinth to provide support to the believers. Saul moved on to Ephesus, where he met some of the Lord's followers. He enquired if they were given the Holy Spirit when they put their trust in Lord Jesus. They confessed that they never even heard of the Holy Spirit.

Not being given to subtleties, Saul accosted them as to why they were baptized. They replied that they were baptized in the name of John the Baptist. Saul gave them a brief history of the Baptist's advice on Lord Jesus. Promptly they were baptized in Jesus Name. Then Saul placed his hands on them and the Holy Spirit came upon them, and they rejoiced and praised the Lord in diverse languages as it happened at Pentecost.

Saul continued to attend worship services at the Yehudic meeting place and bravely expounded the good news of Lord Jesus. This he did over a three months. He tried to win them over, but some of them fiercely resisted and refused to believe. Moreover, they insulted Saul and his message on Lord Jesus right in the presence of the assembled congregation. Saul had left, taking with him the Lord's followers to the lecture hall of Tyrannus. Saul continued daily his ministry there for two years. Perhaps, strategically, it was a right move as the Tyrannus Theatre was a public space. Many Hellenists, Greeks and Yehudes in Asia could freely and without offence to any hierarchy join the crowd and listen to Saul speak on Lord Jesus.

- The Sons of Sceva the High Priest

Empowered by God's unction, Saul worked many miracles of benefit for the needy. Some folks even took the handkerchiefs and aprons that were in contact with Saul's body. They used them to touch everyone who was sick in their healing ministry. All of the sick people who were touched by the garments during the prayers of healing were indeed healed. Even the evil spirits departed from the demoniacs.

Some travelling Jewish exorcists imitated and competed by trying to dispel evil from persons using Jesus Name as did Saul. Seven sons of Sceva, the high priest at the Yehudic meeting place were competing with one another if they could cast out the demons–a pale imitation! An evil spirit responded that it knew who Jesus was! It knew of Saul! But who were they? Then the demoniac jumped on the sons of Sceva and severely bruised them and they ran out of the building bruised and naked.

[Use of formularies were/are common around the world. What results the formulae themselves had were unknown. Faith on the part of the respondent may have played a significant role]

The Sceva story became known among the Hellenistic Yehudes and the Greeks at Ephesus. They were very scared. Consequently, they placed their hope in Lord Jesus. Many who were followers of the Lord confessed their own failures and shortcomings. Some of them who had even practiced sorcery and witchcraft brought their books and burned them in public. The books which were burnt were expensive, worth about fifty thousand silver coins! Some scribes probably made a huge profit. However, the message of Lord Jesus spread rapidly and became all encompassing. (*Probably they were scared straight*)

- The Silversmiths riot at Ephesus

After all of the Sceva related competition, Saul as was his custom felt moved by the Spirit to revisit Macedonia and Achaia before going to Jerusalem, probably also to gain approval from congregations in diverse communities about his proposed trip to Rome. Saul had informed Timothy and Erastus about his proposed visit to Rome from Jerusalem. So he sent his two helpers, to Macedonia, but he still travelled around visiting the followers of the Lord in West Asia for awhile. The newly converted followers needed encouragement and counsel. Perhaps, Saul's strategy of staying with the new Christians for awhile was a wise one.

During that time there were serious troubles for the Lord's followers. They were harassed and persecuted. Demetrius, a silversmith had a prosperous business making silver models of the temple of the goddess Artemis. The silversmiths who worked with Demetrius gained much profit. He realised that conversions to Jesus Way would impact negatively on his business.

Demetrius got together many of those in the same business and said persuasively that while the guild of silversmiths were making reasonable profit through sale of silver artefacts, the stranger in town was trying to convert the people to Jesus Way and away from goddess Artemis. Saul's approach would impact the silversmith business. Saul was going around upsetting many people not only in Ephesus but everywhere in Asia. Saul considered that the images were not conducive to reverence to divinity.

Demetrius argued that those who listened to Saul would start questioning the silversmith business. They would stop honouring and visiting the temple of the goddess Artemis. She was worshiped everywhere in Asia and all over the world. If the people were persuaded to Jesus Way, the great goddess would be forgotten.

Demetrius achieved his end. His workers and other silversmiths got upset and started shouting: "Great is Artemis, the goddess of Ephesus!" Soon thereafter, the whole city was in an uproar. Some men grabbed Gaius and Aristarchus of Macedonia who had accompanied Saul. There was commotion and confusion. The crowd made it to the place where the meetings were held.

Saul the scholar of rhetoric wanted to get out and persuade the crowd. Fortunately, the Lord's followers would not let him out. Some of the bureaucrats who became well disposed towards Saul, also hurriedly sent someone to warn Saul not to get out but to stay put indoors.

Typical of mob-mentality, some of the people shouted one thing and others something else. There was utter chaos and confusion, and most of the crowd didn't even know why they were there in the first place!

Finding the situation as advantageous to their cause with so much antagonism towards Saul, several of the Hellenistic Yehudic residents decided upon getting one Alexander to speak to the crowd. He motioned with his hand and tried to explain what was going on. This back-fired! When the crowd realized that Alexander was a Yehude they went berserk. For two hours, they yelled that Artemis was the great goddess of the Ephesians.

It took a city-bureaucrat to quieten down the crowd. He remarked that the citizen of Ephesus and everyone in the world knew that Ephesus was the center for honouring the great goddess Artemis. The whole world knew that her image fell from heaven right there. Could anyone deny all that?

Not at all, retorted the bureaucrat. Then he ordered them to calm down!

The silversmiths, had brought in a couple of visitors to their great city, who had neither robbed their temples nor spoken against their goddess. The bureaucrat continued that if Demetrius the silversmith and his co-workers had any thing substantive against the visitors, did they not have courts and judges to handle them? He indicated that Demetrius and his colleagues should take their grievances to the courts. However, if they desired to do something ideologically more radical, then, the matter would have to be brought before their city council. The bureaucrat warned that for failing the simple procedural protocol they could be charged with causing a riot that day. There was no excuse for their uproar. After such persuasive reasoning, he dismissed the crowd.

ACTS 20

Saul rejects advice of many leaders not to go to Jerusalem because of his deep convictions

- Saul goes through Macedonia and Greece in his mission journey

Saul over stayed his welcome. After the City Council at Ephesus had provided protection from the mob attack, he was advised to leave. Saul called on the followers of the Lord and said good-bye to them and left for Macedonia. It was difficult for Saul to let go of his leadership and attempts at encouraging the spiritual growth and maturation of the congregations already established. He moved from place to place, and felt the urge to encourage the followers with his exhortations. Where he could not go he wrote letters instead to the Christian communities and sent them out by 'couriers.'

Finally, Saul landed at Corinth in Greece and stayed there for three months, perhaps because he could not find a ship sailing to Syria. When he found a ship, he was about to get on board for his journey to Syria. He learned of some Yehudic plot to nab him. Hence he was forced to take a ship to return by way of Macedonia, to escape getting killed. His work was not yet finished.

Saul was good at gaining friends among the converts and welcoming them to join him in his mission trips. Many of them were only glad to join the man who led them to Lord Jesus. In this escape route, Saul was to be accompanied by Sopater, son of Pyrrhus from Berea, Aristarchus and Secundus from Thessalonica, Gaius from Derbe and Timothy and the two Asians, Tychicus and Trophimus. While Saul had to dodge getting killed from a certain Yehudic plot, he asked his companions to go ahead and wait or him at Troas which they did. After the Festival of Passover, Saul most likely journeyed by land to Philippi. He stayed at Philippi for five days before heading out to Troas. At Troas he was joined by his team who had arrived there earlier and they stayed there for a week.

- Saul's last visit to Troas

On Saturday evening they met together to dine and celebrate the Eucharist. Saul kept on preaching until midnight as he was leaving the next morning. In the upstairs room where they were meeting, there were a lot of lamps and it must have been very warm. A young man Eutychus was sitting on a window sill. While Paul kept on preaching, Eutychus got drowsy, fell asleep and fell three floors down to the street level. When they picked him up, he looked like he was dead. Saul went down and bent over Eutychus, probably measuring his pulse! He took Eutychus in his arms and had pronounced that the young man was alive and they were not to worry! After they all went back upstairs they ate some food. Saul carried on his exhortations until dawn and then left to board a ship. The followers of the Lord had taken Eutychus home alive. They were very happy.

- Saul's voyage from Troas to Miletus

To avoid any unforeseen trap from his antagonists, Saul took the land route to Assos, while the rest of the team went ahead by ship, hoping to be joined by Saul. Saul made it to Assos by road and joined the rest there and they sailed on to Mitylene. The ship reached Chios the next day and the following day the ship made it to Samos. The next day they sailed southeast to Miletus.

Saul was determined to be at Jerusalem for the Feast of Pentecost, hence he bypassed Ephesus, to avoid spending more time in Asia. He was in a hurry and wanted to be in Jerusalem in time for Pentecost as it was customary among the Yehudic people in those days to spend the Feast of Pentecost at the Jerusalem temple.

- From Miletus Saul says good-bye to Church leaders of Ephesus

All the same, Saul wished to meet the Ephesian church leaders *en route* from Miletus. He had sent a message in advance for them to meet him at Miletus. The Ephesian leaders of the Lord's followers made it to Miletus and met with Saul and his team. Saul briefed them that they were aware of all the things he had accomplished, during the time he was with them since he first came to Asia. Saul reaffirmed about the Yehudic plot which had caused much trouble. All the same, Saul served the Lord Jesus in a humble manner both in public and private at different homes which could encourage and help them in Lord Jesus Way. He had the same words for both the Hellenistic Yehudes and the Greeks, namely, to turn to God and have faith in Lord Jesus.

Saul sounded somewhat depressed on what awaited him at Jerusalem. Saul had felt that he must obey the Holy Spirit's voice and go to Jerusalem. He confessed that in every city he had been, he was informed by the Holy Spirit that trouble awaited him at Jerusalem. He might be imprisoned. Saul felt compelled to complete the work that the Lord Jesus had given him to accomplish and proclaim the great kindness of God.

Acts 20

Saul felt in his heart that he would never see the followers of the Lord in Asia again. He had warned that henceforth the leaders were to carry on and encourage the Lord's followers as the Holy Spirit guided them. They could not depend upon his continued guidance. He had done whatever he could do. It was their turn now.

Saul went on exhorting the local leaders to become shepherds to God's church. It was the flock for which Lord Jesus had suffered, died and rose again, therefore they had to be on guard! After he had gone, false teachers would come like fierce wolves to attack them. Under persecution and pressure, some of their own people would tell lies to win over the Lord's followers. They had to remind themselves of the warnings that Saul had given them over three years with tears.

Saul in an emotional manner comforted that his words might be of some help to them. He wished that the Lord grant them, what were the rights of God's peoples. Saul gave witness to his own life-style. He took no money or any wardrobe as wages. As a carpenter, Saul had laboured for his and his companions' keep. He had helped people who were weak. He reminded them of the Lord's saying that more blessings come from giving than from receiving.

After his remarks, Saul, along with the Lord's followers knelt down and prayed. Everyone shed tears and hugged and kissed Saul. They were terribly upset to learn that they would never see him again as he had forewarned. They all went with him to the ship to see him off.

ACTS 21

Saul gets to Jerusalem, visits James, gets into the Temple and is arrested

- Saul goes to Jerusalem in spite of many a plea not to

Saul and his team after the final taking leave, headed to the port and caught a ship sailing south to Cos and thence to Rhodes, which they reached the next day. From Rhodes they sailed on to Patara.

From Patara they boarded a ship that was headed for Phoenicia. The ship passed by Cyprus and sailed south toward Tyre, a large port city in Syria. At Tyre, while the ship was unloading much cargo, Saul and his companions got in touch with the Lord's followers at Tyre and spent a week with them.

The Holy Spirit had warned the Lord's followers at Tyre that Saul should not attempt to get to Jerusalem (*as there was much antagonism against him and it was not the right time*). A week later, the team were on their way again. All the Lord's followers at Tyre, men and women and children, walked with them from the city to the seashore. Before getting on board, Saul and all the Lord's followers who walked with him to the ship, knelt on the beach and prayed. After saying good-bye to one another, the Lord's followers returned home and Saul and the team got back on board about to sail to Ptolemais. At Ptolemais, there was another stop-over for loading and unloading cargo. Saul and his team met with the Lord's followers resident at Ptolemais and stayed over night with them.

From Ptolemais they moved on to Caesarea and stayed with Philip, the evangelist and Apostle. Philip had four unmarried (*virgin*) daughters who were gifted preachers. At Caesarea, Saul and team camped down for several days. Agabus the exhorter-evangelist arrived from Judaea and borrowed Saul's belt and tied it up around his own hands and feet. Then he said that the Holy Spirit had warned that some of the Yehudic leaders in Jerusalem would arrest the owner of the belt and will hand him over to the Roman rulers. After hearing Agabus, the resident followers of the Lord earnestly pleaded with Saul not to enter Jerusalem.

Saul responded that they had better stop crying and breaking his heart. He was ready and willing to be arrested and committed to prison for the sake of Lord Jesus. He would even be prepared to be put to death at Jerusalem! Seeing that Saul would not change his mind, the Lord's followers simply gave up trying. Instead they resorted to prayer that the Lord would guide them to do his will.

Saul and the other followers of the Lord including those from Caesarea got ready to go to Jerusalem. On reaching Jerusalem they were welcomed into the home of Mnason. He was a Hellenistic Yehude from Cyprus and had been a follower of the Lord from the beginning.

- Saul visits James at Jerusalem

The Lord's followers at Jerusalem were glad to welcome Saul and the others who accompanied him from Caesarea when they arrived. The next day, Saul paid a visit to James, the brother of our Lord. All the church leaders, from among the Yehudes turned Christians were present. Saul had greeted them and briefed them on how God had used him among the Gentiles (*i.e., the Hellenists and possibly a few non-Yehudic Greeks*).

Everyone who listened to Saul praised God; and addressed him as a dear friend! They were quick to point out to Saul how tens of thousands of the Yehudes had become followers of Lord Jesus! However, they also were eager to obey the Yehudic rituals of the ancient *Sage*. Some of the Jerusalem Jewish followers of Lord Jesus informed Saul that they had been told that he was teaching those who lived among the Gentiles to disobey the ancient Yehudic rituals. Those converts had allegedly claimed that Saul had instructed them that it was unnecessary to circumcise their sons or to follow the Yehudic customs.

They expected repercussions now that the Jerusalem followers of the Lord had heard that Saul the detractor was in town. The Jerusalem Yehudic Christian leaders advised Saul to join with four others who were going to shave off their hair and do other ritualistic actions. Let Saul pay the cost for him and the other four. Thus everyone would learn that the reports about him were not true and that he had followed all the Yehudic rituals. They reminded Saul of the original contract about non-Yehudic converts. The non-Jewish converts were instructed not to eat anything offered to idols. They were told not to eat any meat from strangled creatures. They were also told not to commit any terrible sexual sins.

The next day Saul took the four men with him and got himself readied, at the same time as the other four did. The five of them went into the temple and made the offerings for each of them. It was an onerous seven day wait to offer their sacrifices.

- Saul was arrested

When some of the Yehudic pilgrims from Asia recognized Saul in the temple, they got whipped-up and worked a large crowd. The crowd started attacking Saul. They started the gossip that Saul was belittling the Yehudic Nation, the temple and the ancient ritual requirements. He had even brought shame to the holy temple by bringing in Gentiles. They had assumed that Saul's companion Trophimus from Ephesus had entered the temple.

The city was in an uproar because they noted that Saul the renegade follower of Jesus was back in Jerusalem. To add to his problems, Saul tended to be upfront and not too discreet. The people turned into a mob. They grabbed Paul and dragged him out of the temple. Then suddenly the doors were shut. The mob was going to lynch Saul. Fortunately for Saul, the Roman commandant of the Garrison had heard that all Jerusalem was in an uproar. He quickly took some soldiers and officers and ran to where the crowd had gathered ready to dispense mob justice.

As soon as the mob saw the commandant and soldiers, they stopped beating Saul. The army commander went over and arrested Saul and had him bound with two chains. Then he tried to find out who Saul was and what he had done. Part of the crowd shouted one thing, and part of them accused him of something else. There was so much noise that the commandant could not find out a thing. Then he ordered his soldiers to take Saul into the fortress. As they reached the steps, the crowd became so wild that the soldiers had to lift Saul up and carry him. The crowd followed and kept shouting to have Saul killed.

- **Saul speaks to the Jewish crowd**

When Saul was about to be taken into the fortress, he had asked the commander in Greek whether he could have a word with him. The surprised commandant enquired as to Saul's ability to communicate in Greek. He had assumed that Saul must have been one of the rabble-rousers. Saul said that he was a Yehude from Tarsus, an important city in Cilicia and that he had wished to speak to the crowd.

The commander gave permission and Saul standing on the steps and motioned to the crowd. When there was silence Saul had addressed the crowd in Aramaic. (*As the crowd were probably Aramaic Jews, this was a wise move to speak to them in their own language rather than in Greek*)

ACTS 22

Saul was saved by the Roman commandant at Jerusalem garrison for protection of Saul from angry mob perhaps stirred up by the Yehudic leadership

Continuation of Saul's speaking to the crowd

Saul urged the friends and leaders of the Jewish Nation to listen to his explanation of what took place. Hearing Saul speaking in Aramaic the crowd quietened down. Saul became oratorical.

He spoke of how he was a Jew born and raised in the city of Tarsus in Cilicia, had studied under the renowned *Rebe* Gamaliel. He had meticulously followed the ancient traditions of the Jews. He was just as eager to obey God as those present there that day.

Saul claimed that he had harassed everyone who was a follower of Lord Jesus Way. He had even beaten some of the Lord's followers and had them charged in front of the high-priests. He confessed that he even had some of the Lord's followers killed. Others, he had arrested and thrown into jail. He was not making any gender distinction between men and women.

Saul went on to say that the high priest and all the Council members could testify to the veracity of his claims. He said that the high priests even gave him letters of endorsement to their counterparts in Damascus that he could arrest and bring the followers of Lord Jesus to Jerusalem to be tried by the Council and be punished.

Saul then gave a brief account of his own conversion. About noon one day, he was about to reach Damascus to arrest the followers of Lord Jesus to be brought to the Jerusalem Temple Council. Suddenly, a bright light flashed around him and his companions. He fell down. There was an accompanying voice addressing him in personal terms asking why he was so determined to ruthlessly persecute Him. Saul queried as to who was talking to him. There came a prompt answer that it was Jesus from Nazareth! He was the one Saul was so cruel to. Saul mellowed and asked what he should do. Then he was advised by the same voice to get up and enter Damascus where he would receive further instructions.

As a result of the brightness of the flash of light, Saul was partially blinded hence the other men had to lead him by hand into Damascus. The companions had seen the bright light, but did not hear the voice. In Damascus, there lived Ananias, a devout follower of Jesus, who however had faithfully kept up with the scruples and rituals of the Yehudes. Consequently, all the Yehudic compatriots and the other citizens respected and liked Ananias. He went out to meet Saul and told him that he would regain his sight. There and then some thing like scales fell off Saul's eyes and he regained sight.

Then Ananias instructed Saul about faith in Lord Jesus, who had spoken to him on his way into Damascus. He had to put his faith in Jesus and be baptized in Jesus name and then he had to bear witness to everybody of what he had seen and heard. Ananias told Saul to rise up and get baptized to wash away his sins. After his baptism, Saul returned to Jerusalem and went to the temple to pray. There he had a vision of the Lord ordering to get out of Jerusalem quickly. As can be expected of Saul, he had argued with the Lord about his past fierce zeal for Yehudism (*prior to his conversion*) which should mollify the Jerusalem crowd. He had been even a witness to Stephen's murder. He had beaten up the followers of Jesus. But the Lord had firmly pointed out that the Jerusalem Yehudes were not prepared to hear from Saul.

Apparently, the Lord had insisted on Saul's immediate departure from Jerusalem. He also promised Saul to be sent far away as his news-bearer to the (*learned*) Greeks (*Gentiles*). The Yehudic crowd listened quietly to Saul till he had made the claim about his proposed ministry among the Greeks. Then they rioted and shouted for Saul's murder. They yelled that Saul did not deserve to live and they kept on yelling. As a sign of their strong protest the crowd waved their outer garments. Some of the riff-raff threw hands-full of dust into the air.

- Saul and the Roman Army Commandant

As the yelling and screaming continued, the Roman Commandant of the garrison decided to bring Saul into the fort to avoid any violence from occurring. He wanted to ascertain from Saul as to why there was so much commotion over him.

While the soldiers were tying up Saul to be beaten, he had asked the officer standing there, whether it was right to beat-up a Roman citizen before he had been legally tried in a court of law. When the officer heard this, he went to the commandant and told him that Saul was a Roman citizen and he had not been through due process.

The commandant went over to Saul and asked whether he was a Roman citizen. Saul affirmed. The commandant commented that he had paid a lot of money (*probably legally and through bribery*) to become a Roman citizen. Paul countered that he was a Roman citizen by birth. The men who were preparing to ascertain the truth about Saul and the commotion backed-off. And the commandant became nervous when he realized that he had put a Roman citizen in chains without due process.

- Saul was tried by the Jerusalem Jewish Council

On the next day, the commandant ordered the chief priests and the whole Yehudic Council to meet in his presence and bring charges against Saul. He had his soldiers remove the chains from Saul who was in the lock-up in a jail-cell; and he brought Saul out to answer to any charges levied against him by the Yehudic leadership.

ACTS 23

The Commandant brought Saul to the Jewish Council for trial before a wild crowd

Saul looked straight at the Council members and solemnly claimed that he had been serving God, conscientiously for many years. Then Ananias the high priest ordered the men standing beside Saul to slap him for mouthing. Saul turned to the high priest and called him a white-washed wall (*i.e., someone who pretended to be good but really wasn't*) and that God would punish him. Saul boldly accused Ananias of being seated to judge him by the Yehudic laws and traditions yet breaking the traditions by ordering someone to slap him. Those standing beside Saul remarked that he was insulting God's high priest.

Saul apologized and said that he was unaware that Ananias was the high priest. He affirmed that the Yehudic scriptures clearly stated that the followers of the Yehudic traditions could not and should not insult a leader of the people.

Being an extremely astute person, Saul saw an opportunity emerge to confound the process. Saul noted that some of the councillors were Sadducees and others were Pharisees. He made it quite clear that he was a Pharisee; the son of a Pharisee; and he was on trial simply because he believed that the dead would be raised to life.

Saul's one sentence had the desired effect. The Pharisees and the Sadducees got into a big argument; and the council members started taking sides. The Sadducees did not believe in angels or spirits or that the dead would rise to life. (*In practice* however, *the Sadducees were secularists*) The Pharisees believed in all of the evolving strict rules and there was a great argument emerging between the two sects. Some of the teachers of the Yehudic laws were Pharisees. They were frustrated and claimed that they did not find anything wrong with the man. The qualifier was that perhaps a spirit or an angel must have spoken to Saul.

The argument between the Pharisees and Sadducees became fierce that the commandant was worried that Saul would be torn apart. He ordered the soldiers to go in and rescue Saul. The soldiers took Saul back into the fort. Saul was assured by the Lord not to be concerned. Just as he had stood up for His cause at Jerusalem he would do so at Rome.

- A Jewish plot to kill Saul

The spirit of antagonism and revenge among the Yehudic community was so great that the next morning more than forty men met together and vowed to have Saul murdered and that they would neither eat nor drink till they fulfilled their murderous avowal. Some of them met with the chief priests and the other Council members to inform them of their vows. They recommended that the Councillors should ask the Roman Commandant to have Saul brought before their Council so that they would have another go at finding more about Saul's ideologies and activities which caused the riot. If they could manage to persuade the Commandant to let Saul be brought to Jerusalem Jewish Court, they would lie in wait and have him murdered *en route* to their court.

Rumour spread and Saul's nephew learned about the plot, and he rushed to the fortress and contacted Saul about the plot. Saul requested one of the garrison officers to let his nephew speak to the commandant as he had something important to confide to him. The duty officer obliged and took the young man to the commandant. The commandant took Saul's nephew aside and enquired what he had to say to him.

Saul's nephew blew the whistle on the secret plot being devised by the Yehudic Council to call for further questioning of Saul the next morning. He narrated the plan of the plot on how Saul would be ambushed and killed *en route* to the Jerusalem Jewish Council Chambers from the Fort. The young man pleaded with the garrison commandant to protect Saul. There were forty or more men waiting to kill Saul vowing that they would neither eat nor drink till Saul was murdered. Indeed they were waiting to hear the commandant's decision. After hearing from the young man, the commandant sent him away advising him not to talk to anyone about the interview.

- Saul was sent to Felix the Governor

Immediately, the commandant ordered two of his officers to have two companies of soldiers ready to take Saul to Caesarea by nine o'clock that night. He had instructed that seventy cavalry men (*on horseback*) and two hundred foot soldiers with spears were to leave with Saul on horse back to ensure that Saul reached Caesarea safely to report to the Roman governor Felix. Claudius Lysias, the commandant wrote a brief summary of the emergent situation.

It said that Claudius Lysias was sending greetings to the Honorable Governor Felix. It briefed Felix that some Jews had grabbed the accused man and were about to kill him. When Lysias had found out that Saul was a Roman citizen, he had taken some soldiers and rescued him and would wish to examine what the Yehudic crowd had against him.

Hence he had brought him, before the Jewish Council and had learned that the charges had something to do with their religious laws. Lysias found that the man was not guilty of anything for which he should be put to death or even be jailed. Furthermore, he had learned that there was a plot against him to kill him. Therefore he was sending him to Felix. Lysias had already informed the Yehudic leaders to take their charges against the man directly to the Governor at Caesarea.

The soldiers carried out the commandant's orders, and that very night Saul was taken to Antipatris for the next stage of the journey to Caesarea by cavalry men. The next day the two companies of the foot soldiers had returned to the fortress. The cavalrymen carried on the rest of the way with Saul on horseback. When they arrived at the garrison at Caesarea, they handed Saul over with the note from the Jerusalem garrison commandant.

After reading the note from Lysias, the governor talked to Saul and found out that he was from Cilicia. He informed Saul that he would wait till his accusers had arrived at Caesarea to present their complaints. After his conversation with Saul, Governor Felix ordered that Saul be kept in lock-up at the Herod's palace.

[The Palace at Caesarea most probably was built by Herod the Great. However, it was used by the Roman governors of Palestine. Such insensitive actions by the colonial governments of the Roman Empire only further irritated the Jewish people who had resented the Roman dominance]

ACTS 24

Saul brought before Felix the governor at Caesarea under heavy guard

- Saul was accused in the Court of Governor Felix

Ananias, the high priest, together with some of the Jerusalem Yehudic leaders and Tertullus their lawyer arrived in Caesarea five days later. Tertullus, the prosecuting lawyer presented the case against Saul before Governor Felix. Tertullus had opened his case with great adulation for the fair-mindedness of Felix. He had further requested Felix to kindly bear with the Jewish delegation, just for a few minutes to hear their complaint.

With that opening courtesy, Tertullus went on a vicious attack against Saul. He accused Saul of being a trouble-maker among the Yehudic communities all over the Empire. Saul was also a leader of a group known as *Nazarenes*. He tried to desecrate the Jerusalem temple, hence he was arrested. The Yehudic Council would have dealt with him judiciously, but for Lysias the commandant of the Jerusalem garrison. Lysias used force to remove him from justice being meted out by their court system. Then Lysias ensured that Saul was sent to Caesarea the provincial capital for trial before Felix the governor. Lysias the commandant ordered the plaintiffs to make their case in the provincial court hence, Tertullus and the Yehudic delegation arrived in Caesarea. Upon hearing such a presentation, the Yehudic crowd murmured their agreement with Tertullus oration before Governor Felix.

- Saul's self defence

When Tertullus ended his prosecution case, the governor motioned for Saul to make his defence. Saul did not have a defence lawyer (*probably he could not afford one; and did not want one either!*). He spoke for himself. He began his defence by affirming what Tertullus had said, namely that under Felix the Roman governor, there was peace and fairness of treatment of the Yehudic people of Judaea and Samaria and that he was glad to be given the opportunity to defend himself in front of the governor.

Saul made his defence, step by step. Approximately twelve days ago he had gone to worship in Jerusalem. He pointed out that he did not argue with anyone in the temple, or cause any commotion in the Yehudic meeting places or in the city itself. He unequivocally affirmed that he was a follower of Lord Jesus Way, which some of the Yehudic leaders considered as based on wrong beliefs. Saul was still worshiping the same God that his forebears had worshiped and that he believed in the Yehudic sacred literature.

As a partisan strategist, Saul threw in his claims on resurrection of the dead and judgement. Because of his surety, he tried to follow his conscience in everything he did for God or fellow men. After he had been away for many years, he had returned to Jerusalem with donations for the Yehudic poor people; and to offer his ritualistic offerings at the temple. He was not in contact with any of the crowd at the temple and that there had been no uproar either.

Saul mentioned that there were some Hellenistic Yehudes from the province of Asia present during his visit to the temple. None of them seemed to be present (*at the Caesarea Court*) with the accusing crowd. Saul turned the table against the accusers through his defence. The Hellenists could confirm for Felix if he was rude or obnoxious when he was tried by the Jewish Council at Jerusalem. He did reaffirm that he had shouted out in the Jerusalem Jewish Court that he was on trial for his belief that the dead would be raised to life.

Felix the governor knew much about Jesus Way and its followers hence, he did not need further elaborations. Felix's spouse Drusilla was a Yehudic lady. Felix adjourned the court and announced that he would reassemble the court after the arrival of Lysias, the Jerusalem garrison commandant. He had reserved his judgement till then. Felix ordered the army officer to keep Saul under guard but not to lock him up. Saul could have visitors while waiting for Lysias.

- Confinement of Saul at Caesarea

Several days later, Felix and his spouse Drusilla, visited Saul kept under guard. They listened to Saul talk about having faith in Lord Jesus. Governor Felix was somewhat dismayed to hear Saul talking to them about doing right, self-control, and the coming judgment. He dismissed Saul back to the guard house. But he alerted Saul that he would send for him to listen more when he had some time. It was possible that Felix may also have had expected some bribes from Saul. Alas! Saul was a pauper.

This went on for two years. No doubt Saul was out of circulation, but he could still have visitors and write briefs to the Christian communities that he had helped establish or that were already established by the Lord's followers, among whom Saul had ministered.

Two years later, while Saul was still constrained in the guard house in Caesarea, Felix was replaced by a new governor Porcius Festus. Felix and Drusilla wishing to mollify the Jewish establishment had left Saul in detention when they moved on to another appointment.

ACTS 25

Saul defends himself in front of Felix and Festus at Caesarea and found not guilty and would have been released but for his appeal to the Roman Emperor

- Saul appealed for trial before the Roman Emperor

After becoming the governor, Festus, had heard of the complaints against Saul from the Jerusalem Yehudic establishment. Saul was rescued by his predecessor Felix and had been left in jail at Caesarea. He had been briefed on the circumstances hence he avoided yielding to the request of Yehudic leadership to order Saul to be taken to Jerusalem. He had suggested to the complainants that they could brief him about their charges on his visit to Jerusalem in three days.

Governor Festus' visit to Jerusalem lasted more than eight to ten days before his return to the provincial capitol Caesarea. Back in Caesarea Festus took his seat at the bench (court) and Saul was brought in. As soon as Saul was brought in, the Yehudic leaders from Jerusalem had crowded around him and shouted that he was guilty of many serious crimes. They did not provide any legitimate proof. Then Saul was asked to respond in self-defence. Saul maintained that he had not broken any of the ancient Yehudic ritualistic laws or, had he done anything against the Jerusalem temple or, the Emperor.

In order to accommodate the request of the Yehudic leadership, Festus had asked Saul whether he would be prepared to be tried by him at Jerusalem on the charges brought up against him. Saul knew what would happen if he yielded ground – he would be murdered! He stuck to his strategy. He categorically affirmed that he was on trial at the Emperor's court and that was where he should be tried. He also maintained that he had done nothing to harm the Yehudic nation. If he had indeed done something wrong worthy of a death sentence, he would not try to avoid such a penalty. He was not guilty of any crime hence no one should hand him over to the complainants. Then he proceeded to plead that he be tried by the Emperor himself.

Festus then consulted with the complainants, the members of the Jerusalem Yehudic Council and informed Saul that since he had asked for trial by the Emperor, he would be sent to the Emperor.

- Saul given opportunity to address King Agrippa and his consort Bernice

King Agrippa II (*son the Agrippa I, and great-grandson to Herod the Great*) was the procurator of Jerusalem. He and his consort Bernice decided to visit Festus the governor of Caesarea and stayed with him for several days. Festus told them about Saul and the complaints against him from the Jerusalem Yehudic Council.

Agrippa and Bernice were briefed on Saul being left in prison by his predecessor Felix. Felix had mentioned about the complaints of the Jerusalem Yehudic leadership against Saul; and how a riot had broken out. To protect the accused from harm, Felix had left Saul in jail and was in the process of trying him. When the accusers pressed their charges it

Acts 25

was not any of the crimes that would result in any serious penalties.

The Yehudic leaders argued with him at the trial about some of their beliefs and about a dead man named Jesus who Saul had claimed was alive. But seeing that the Jewish mob was about to take over, Felix had Saul removed by force by the soldiers and kept in prison.

The Yehudic leaders came to Caesarea for the trial. They wanted to try him at their Court in Jerusalem. To accommodate their request, Felix had asked Saul whether he would be willing to go to Jerusalem and be tried by him there. But Saul had asked to be kept in jail until the Emperor could decide his case. So he had ordered Saul to be kept in the local prison until the Governor could send him to the Emperor.

Agrippa also wanted to hear Saul. Festus arranged for Agrippa to hear Saul the next day. Agrippa and Bernice came out to the meeting in great splendour. They had some of the top army commanders and important citizens of the town present in the room. Festus then ordered Saul to be brought in. Festus pointing at Saul said to King Agrippa and the others that all the Jewish people of Jerusalem and Caesarea were demanding that he be put to death. However, Festus did not find Saul guilty of any misdemeanour worthy of death. Saul did not wish to go to Jerusalem for trial by the Yehudic leadership. He had asked to be tried by the Emperor hence Festus was waiting to send him to Rome.

Festus needed some thing to write to the Emperor about the case and that he would be grateful to King Agrippa for any suggestions he may have. After Agrippa had a chance to hear Saul, he and Festus could decide a course of action by way of some charges.

ACTS 26

Agrippa, the great-grandson of Herod the Great and consort Bernice listen to Saul

- King Agrippa and consort Bernice were impressed by Saul's defence

King Agrippa asked Saul to speak-up. With out-stretched arms Saul spoke in self defence against all the charges brought against him by the Yehudic leaders. He was glad to defend himself before the King who had much knowledge about the Yehudic religion, its customs and traditions and that which divided them. Saul had asked for a patient hearing.

The Yehudic people had known Saul since he was a child and what kind of life-style he was leading in his native Cilicia and at Jerusalem and his commitment for the Yehudic faith. If the accusers were willing, they themselves could tell Agrippa about him; and that he was a Pharisee. The Pharisees were stricter in following Yehudic traditions than any other groups of Yehudes. Saul claimed that he was arrested and was now standing trial because of his profound faith in the promises God had made to his people in times past. Along with them he too had hoped for God's blessings. Saul, the rhetorician, addressed King Agrippa claiming that he was

Acts 26

on trial for his hope of the resurrection of the dead. It was no doubt a legitimate belief that God raised the dead to life.

Saul gave a brief summary of his life history. He was angry with the followers of Lord Jesus; and that he was on the look-out to arrest them in foreign cities with letters of approval from the Jerusalem Yehudic establishment. He talked about his conversion experience and later fiery defence of Jesus Way. Jesus had ordered him to bear witness to him and that he would protect him from both the Yehudes and the Gentiles. He followed the challenge and was arrested and was waiting for trial before the Emperor.

Saul went on reciting all his activities. Before Saul had finished defending himself, Festus shouted out that Saul was talking in a crazy manner and that his great scholarship had driven him out of his mind. Saul took the remark coolly and retorted that he had not gone crazy. The events actually took place in public and not in some little village or town. Saul the lawyer continued his defence boldly by saying that the King knew what he was talking about. He further challenged the King whether he believed in the traditions of the Yehudic *Sages*. Saul had further maintained that the King did indeed believe.

King Agrippa had enough of it. He retorted that Saul was trying to make him a follower of Jesus in such a brief time, with his oratory. Saul would not give up. He suggested that whether it took a short time or long time, he would love to see everyone believe like himself except that they should not have to be chained like he was!

King Agrippa, Governor Festus, Bernice, and everyone who was with them got up to leave. Before they left they remarked that Saul was not guilty of anything and that he did not deserve to die or be put in prison. Agrippa mentioned to Festus that Saul could be set free had it not been for the fact that he had appealed to the Roman Emperor.

ACTS 27

Saul's journey to Rome slowed amidst storm and ship-wreck

- Paul was being taken by ship to Rome

When the sailing season started, the governor of Caesarea decided to transfer the prisoner to Rome by sea. Captain Julius from the Emperor's special troops was made in-charge of Saul. When it was time to sail to Rome, Captain Julius was put in charge of Saul and the other prisoners. Julius was very kind to Saul. He let Saul have freedom to move about visiting with his friends. They caught a ship from Adramyttium which was headed to some ports along the coast of Asia. Saul's friend Aristarchus from Thessalonica in Macedonia went with Saul on board.

On the next day the ship arrived at Sidon. Captain Julius let Saul's friends visit with him and replenish any goods and services he needed. When the ship left Sidon, the winds were blowing against them, hence the captain decided to try to sail close to the shore line and then to sail close to Cyprus as a protection against heavy winds. Then the ship's captain decided on moving south of Cilicia and Pamphylia till it could reach the port of Myra in Lycia. At Myra the Roman army captain in-charge of Saul and other prisoners found a ship from Alexandria that was headed to Italy. He decided to take his party aboard that vessel.

For several days they were in the stormy sea and the overclouded sky. The trip took several days getting to Cnidus, struggling against the winds and the storms. The winds were fierce and the ship could not move forward. They sailed past Cape Salmone on the south east coast of Cyprus hoping for protection from Crete against the winds. The ship slowly 'drifted' along the coast and finally reached a place called Fair Havens, not far from the town of Lasea on the south coast of Crete.

Since they were delayed so much *en route* to Fairhaven, the sailing season was over and it would have been foolhardy trying to sail safely any further. In fact, even the Great Day of Forgiveness was past.

[It was a Yehudic festival and it took place at the end of September. The sailing season was dangerous after mid-September, and it was stopped completely between the middle of November and middle of March].

As usual, even as a prisoner, Saul invariably provided counsel. He ventured to speak to the crew of the ship and asked them to pay attention to him. If they decided to sail under the windy season, their ship and its cargo would be badly damaged and many lives would be lost. Alas! Understandably, Julius would rather listen to the ship's captain and the ship's owners than to Saul. Furthermore, the harbour at Fair Havens wasn't a safe haven for winter. Based on the harbour conditions, practically all agreed that they should at least try to sail along the coast of Crete as far as Phoenix, where they could spend the winter.

- The development of storm at sea

There developed a gentle wind from the south and the crew decided it could be a chance to carry out their original plan. They hoisted the anchor and sailed along the south coast of Crete moving further westward. Very soon the strong wind 'The Northeaster' blew against the ship from the island! The wind struck the ship in full force and it could not sail into it, hence the captain and crew decided on letting the ship drift along the coast.

They made it past the isle of Cauda (*probably Knosbos*) on the side that was protected from the fierce wind. The crew had a hard time keeping the lifeboat in its hanger. Then the sailors wrapped ropes around the ship to hold it together. They lowered the sail and let the ship drift along; because they were afraid it might hit the sandbanks in the gulf of Syrtis. The storm was so fierce that the next day the crew threw out some of the ship's cargo overboard to lighten the ship. On the third day, the crew dislodged some the ship's gear and rolled them overboard. Nothing worked; and for several days they were in the over-clouded and stormy sea. A strong wind kept blowing, and the crew finally gave up all hope of being saved. Saul the prisoner 'leader,' stood up to comfort all the wearied and worried passengers and crew and begged them to cheer up, because they will be safe. Only the ship would be lost!

Saul and the others on board the ship were drifting at sea for fourteen days and nights blown around the Mediterranean Sea by heavy winds. By about midnight the sailors realized that they were getting near some land mass. They took depth measurements and it was about one hundred twenty feet deep. A little later they found it was only about ninety feet. The crew were afraid that they might hit some rocks if they drifted further. Therefore, the sailors let down four anchors from the stern. Then they all prayed for daylight.

The sailors decided to escape from the ship. So they lowered the lifeboat pretending as if they were heading towards the bow to let down an anchor from the bow. Saul warned Captain Julius and the soldiers that if the sailors didn't stay on board, they would not have any chance to save their lives. The soldiers then cut the ropes that held the lifeboat and let it fall into the sea. Thus the escape of the sailors was averted.

Just before daylight Saul begged everybody to eat something. He reasoned that the people on board should eat some food since none of them had eaten any food for fourteen days, being worried over life and death. He begged them to eat something as their ship-wrecked lives will need some energy. If they ate some food right then, none of them would loose their lives when the ship broke-up and they would be stranded ashore.

After making the plea, Saul took a piece of bread and after giving thanks to God began to eat the bread in front of everybody. The folks on board felt touched, and each of them ate something. There were 276 people on board; and after everyone had eaten, they threw the cargo of wheat into the sea to make the ship even lighter.

- The Shipwreck due to gale force winds

The next morning the ship's crew saw a coast that they were not familiar with. They also saw a cove with a beach. The crew ventured to run the ship aground on the beach. They untied the ropes that were holding the rudders. Next, they hoisted the fore-sail thus permitting the ship to drift to the beach. Alas! The ship ran aground on a sandbank. The front of the ship got stuck deeply in the sand. The rear was being smashed by the force of the waves.

The soldiers for their part were worried that the prisoners would escape by swimming to the shore. Captain Julius wanted to save Saul's life. Therefore, he did not permit the soldiers' easy solutions. Then he told the others to hang on to any planks of wood or parts of the ship. At last, everyone safely reached the shore.

ACTS 28

Saul and party on the Island of Malta; Saul ended-up in a rental house in Rome

- Hazardous Journey to Malta on rough sea

When they arrived ashore they had learnt that the island was called Malta. The people there were very friendly, and welcomed the ship-wrecked people. They built a fire to keep the people warm as it was rainy and cold. Saul joined the crowd to collect drift wood for the fire. He unloaded his pile on to the fire. The heat caused a snake to crawl out and bit Saul on his hand. When the local people saw the snake was still hanging on to Saul, they wondered that must be a murderer because in spite of the fact that he escaped ship-wreck, the goddess of justice would not let him escape justice.

Saul simply shook off the snake into the fire and he was unharmed. The Maltese kept looking to see if Saul's hand would swell up or that he would drop dead. They kept watching for a long time, and when nothing terrible happened to him, they changed their minds and proclaimed that the man must be a god.

The ever so friendly governor Publius welcomed the ship-wrecked folks into his home for three days. Publius' father was bed-ridden, sick with some fever and stomach ache. Saul went over to visit him and prayed and placed his hands on the elderly man and healed him.

When those who watched or learned later about Saul's ministry of healing, they rushed out to bring their own sick to be healed by Saul. They were all healed. The people were full of gratitude. When the ship-wrecked folks sailed away in a different ship, the people of Malta brought all the needed victuals and daily necessities for the rest of their journey to Rome after their three month delay.

- Journey from Malta to Rome

Three months later, they sailed in a ship that had been docked at Malta for the winter. On their first port of call Syracuse, the party stayed for three days (*to load victuals and unload goods*). From Syracuse, they sailed off to Rhegium. A south wind was blowing and the party managed to arrive at Puteoli.

At Puteoli, they found some of the Lord's followers who urged them to stay with them for a few days. A week later they finally left for the city of Rome. Some of the followers of the Lord at Rome heard about the apostle turned prisoner being escorted to the Emperor's court, they came out to meet them at the Market of Appius and at the Three Inns. When Saul saw them, he was full of gratitude to God and was very encouraged.

- Paul at Rome

At Rome, Saul was allowed to live in a rented house by himself with a soldier on guard.

After three days of settling down in his rented place, Saul got together some of the Yehudic leaders in the city and informed them of his travails and the vengeful attitude of the Jerusalem Jewish Council despite the Roman governor's decision that he had not found any wrong doing on Saul's part. The governor and King Herod Antipas II would have released him but due to the mob's determination to kill him, Saul had appealed to be tried by the Emperor; and now he was there in their midst.

Saul kept repeating that he was innocent of any wrong doing; he had not contravened any of the ancient Yehudic customs and ritual traditions. In Jerusalem, he was handed over as a prisoner to the Romans. They found that he had not done anything deserving of death. He had not done or said anything against the Yehudic nation. The Yehudic leaders of Jerusalem and Caesarea disagreed and Saul asked the Emperor to try him. The Yehudic hopes were fulfilled and Saul was again bound in chains. He was bound in chains for the very things that the Yehudic people hoped for. Saul wanted the Yehudic communities of Rome to know the reason why he was brought to Rome as a prisoner.

The Yehudic leaders responded that they had no complaints from anybody in Judaea verbally or in writing. There were no Jewish representatives visiting or, saying anything against him. However, they would be glad to listen to what he had to say. They also informed Saul that they had heard that the Yehudic people everywhere were against the new group called the 'Followers of Jesus.'

The Yehudic community leaders in Rome set a time to meet with Saul. Many of them visited with Saul in his rented house to hear what he had to communicate to them. Saul, in his usual manner talked from early morning until late in the afternoon using Yehudic scriptures about God's kingdom trying to persuade them to become followers of Lord Jesus' Way.

There was fierce division among the listeners. Some accepted Saul's arguments while others were not so sure. Due to the division of opinion (*and perhaps due to the lengthy debate*) the Yehudic leaders began to leave. To add to the tense situation Saul became impatient, and started quoting Yehudic scriptures accusing the impatient listeners. Saul ended his first dialogue with his fellow Yehudic people of Rome by saying that God wished also to invite the Gentiles into his circle as followers of Lord Jesus and that the members of the Yehudic community of Rome and its environs should also listen. Saul stayed in his rented house for two years waiting for his hearing in the Emperor's court. In the meanwhile, Saul conversed with any one who came to see him. He spoke of Lord Jesus Way boldly and no one tried to stop him.

Part II
(Covering material not included in the received text of the Acts of the Apostles)

Chapter 29

LIFE-STYLES IN THE FIRST CENTURY ROMAN EMPIRE AND GENTILE CONVERTS TO JESUS WAY

During Saul's time, there was relative freedom of expression in the Roman Empire, perhaps unparalleled in the history of the times. The attempts made by nations and empires at creating an environment of unification among diverse populations of many different religious faith systems often did not work. Knowing the socio-anthropological reality did not (and does not) stop the committed/zealots from trying.

Those who had tried were rewarded for trying. Societies with grain, oil, gas and other resources and/or, financial abundance seem to support the efforts at conversion or, acceptance of various kinds of services (e.g., healthcare, education, economy) towards sub-conscious impact. Any such attempts were often ineffective as some form of religion was/is a core value among human aggregations. Often social and individual ethics manifest in some form of religious Faith.

When enterprising groups or societies tried to use any one religious framework as superior to other Faiths and practices, they had often become triggers for disharmony. In the present Twenty-first century, the major points of division may be subsumed under the attempts at persuasive religious arguments in favour of one Faith against a diversity of Faiths and spirituality. The eighteenth to the twentieth century attempts at 'converting' huge agglomerations of people to some major religious position(s) created problems of dissonance than consonance. Of course, there were success stories too.

The author was at the United Nations Religion Conference at New York in 2001, when a poor/ordinary looking elderly African gentleman got up to address the plenary session, he just stated that the Western Christian religious groups attacked the Western half of Africa while diverse branches of the Islamic Faith attacked the Eastern half. The religions and spirituality practiced by himself and fellow unsophisticated were denigrated and the common folks were left confused and nowhere to turn to.

Power, Pelf and Persuasion became the underpinnings of existence today as ever before! (Lebens-Sitzung)

- A note on Gentile converts towards "universality" of Jesus Way

In his *A History of the Church to AD 461*, B. J. Kidd (Clarendon Press, Oxford 1922. v.1) has highlighted the rift developing between the Jerusalem Jewish Christians and the Hellenized Jewish Christians of the Diaspora. Under Peter's ministry, the gospel began to spread among the Hellenists and among the Samaritans. This meant a move away from Jerusalem to Antioch in Syria, where the newly emerging "Followers of the Jesus Way" were comfortable and felt at home and a release from the dominance of the Jewish

Christians of Jerusalem. It was in Antioch that the followers of Jesus Way were knick named 'Christians'–soldiers of Jesus. The followers of Jesus Way were stuck with the new appellation ever since.

There were problems with the above description. It tied the new faith based religion with Judaism, which was unnecessary for the future of the Church. The most profound problem was that the Incarnation of God becoming human could and indeed had been side stepped and Judaism sneaked in through the back door. The gospel of the Blessed Lord Jesus, the *Yesu Avtar* was often consciously or sub-consciously not the focus of much of the homilies from the pulpit, at least in North America. After two thousand years of propagation of Jesus Way, the church was still stuck in Yehudic rituals and feasts.

- Jesus Way spread like wild fire

One took comfort in the fact that the message of the gospel spread like wild-fire in the Roman Empire, and before the end of the first century of the present era the gospel message spread through much of the Roman Empire, so much so that the Yehudic communities felt threatened and some times reacted vehemently. It was more than plain jealousy. Dr Saul had targeted the Yehudic communities which were well spread and often affluent throughout the Roman world.

Naturally, the already well established Yehudic communities on the Mediterranean shores and on the islands were utterly dismayed, jealous and resentful of the staggering achievements of the 'unlearned' apostles and their disciples 'right under their nose' as it were! The places where the apostles made followers of Lord Jesus included Salamis, Paphos in Cyprus, Malta, Tripoli in Libya, Antioch and Damascus in Syria, Jerusalem, Caesarea, Antioch, Iconium, Lystra, Tarsus, Derbe, Pergamum, Thyatira, Colossae and Myrna in Cappadocia; Puteoli and Rome; and Athens, Aegina, Cenchreae, Corinth, Patrae, Patmos, and Nicopolis in Achea.

The already well established small but often wealthy Jewish communities targeted the apostles, and the followers of Lord Jesus. Saul was especially resented. However, the Yehudic communities had a favourable opinion of the Elder Barnabas of Cyprus. As was noted in Part I, Barnabas was a dignified and gentle soul.

Chapter 30

ADMINISTRATION, WORSHIP, UNITY AND ROLE OF APOLOGISTS WITH CHURCH GROWTH

- Emerging administrative organization as Church grew and expanded

Peter King in his *An Inquiry into the Constitution, Discipline, Unity and Worship of the Primitive Church.* New York. 1851 had maintained that any authority that any Church Courts may have exercised, were based on the promise and commission of Blessed Lord Jesus to build His Church on that rock that would stand. King noted that there was an evolution of the hierarchy of office in the primitive church in the face of expected or already existing persecutions.

Under threats of persecution, many converts had deserted the Church and escaped to other cities, towns, villages and possibly provinces where persecution was not yet in vogue. They suffered excommunication, which in and of itself was a heavy burden to bear as it was a form of intolerable isolationism.

When persecutions subsided, a vast majority of the converts returned and confessed; and were reintegrated with some penalty on the demands made by those who did not desert! If the clergy were the ones who had deserted during persecutions, when they returned they were reintegrated with penalty only as laity. Their priesthood was permanently annulled, and were considered ineligible for such priestly functions. (pp.117ff)

- Emergence of hierarchy in Ministry

The emergence of a hierarchical leadership for administrative purposes had come to stay with the Christian communities. By the second century AD the old approach of each congregation being under its own presbyter-bishop, presbyters and deacons, meeting regularly at least once year or more often as synodical assemblies, was giving way to bishops with jurisdiction over many congregations in a manageably area/district. The bishop and representative presbyters (*many continued the concept of 'priests' in place of the terminology of 'presbyter'*) and deacons and representatives of 'laity' of several congregations became the norm. Initially it was the answer to the problem of travel distance that led to this development. Firmilian, bishop of Caesarea in Cappadocia stated that in his Province they (*the Synod*) met every year. By Cyprian's time, his provincial synod met at least once and some times two or three times. At a synod in Antioch in Syria they condemned Paulus Samosatenus, a bishop. It was evident that at the Antiochean synod all bishops, presbyters, deacons and lay representatives of several congregations were present. This development had come to stay till today.

- Church discipline

Reintegration of the penitent delinquents often required that they had to come in a humble manner, weeping and crying to the church door; where they had to lay grovelling on the ground, prostrating at the feet of the faithful who were entering into the church, pleading for the prayers to God on their behalf. Tertullian in the second century described one such penitential process as lying in sackcloth and ashes, by having squalid body, and a dejected soul, by fasting, praying, weeping, groaning and roaring, night and day; by throwing themselves at the feet of the clergy, and kneeling before the faithful, begging and desiring their prayers and pardon.

- **Saint Cyprian provided certain principles of Unity and Faith**

St. Cyprian in his *De Lapsis* (*Sections 24 and 25 p.-285*) mentioned of a woman who had 'indulged' in worldly life, under persecution deserted. When she returned after persecution was over, she was admonished severely, as to why the wretched woman had lost her soul. She too had to weep bitterly both night and day in tears and lamentations. She needed to prostrate herself upon the ground, and rolling herself in dust and ashes. Such penitential rite may have lasted for days, months, years and even to the end of lifetime. However, such penalties may have been dependent upon the circumstance of the offence, the offender and the pleasure of the ecclesiastical courts. There were no uniform pattern and was cause for concern in Cyprian's time (*pp.121, 22*). It appeared however, that often advice was sought after and given by other congregations in the area. (*p.130*). It was still a time of patriarchal ways!

- **Patterns of Worship**

Justin Martyr on worship and unity of the Church

Justin had recollected that when the community had met for worship, after an opening Prayer by the senior most leader, the reading of the prophets and apostles. (*King p.165*) Besides the apostolic writings, there were public readings of other contemporary epistles, tracts and commentaries of eminent and spiritual leaders. e.g., Pastor (*the book of Hermas*), epistles of Clement of Roman to the Church of Corinth were read aloud in many congregations. The reading or recital (*and hymn singing*) was usually undertaken by the lector (clerk), for whom such public acts were stepping stones towards holy orders.

We learn from Edgar Goodspeed (*A History of early Christian Literature*. revised and enlarged by Robert Grant. 1966), that the earliest Apologies were written at the time, related to the transition of gradual separation of Christianity from Yehudism. They began to feel their distinct history, theology and behavioural norms in a competing ethnic, religious and cultural world of the Roman Empire.

They were also trying to counter the opposition based on ignorance about the new faith and resultant fear and persecution. The Christians were sometimes accused of being incestuous, cannibalistic, atheistic and disloyal, arousing suspicion and hostility. The pagan philosopher Tacitus saw the Christian worship as cannibalism and the Christians were 'haters of humanity'. Tacitus claimed that to the official hostility of the government were added the suspicion and detestation of the Roman public (*Annals xv.44*). While Nero might have set fire to public places for his own entertainment, he and his supporters could blame the Christians who were practising a religion which was not approved by the Emperor (*religio illicita*).

The Apologists were explaining the beliefs and practice of the Christians. While they did not offer sacrifice to the statues of the Emperor (*a pinch of incense thrown into the fire in front of the statues of the Emperor which were cropping up all over the empire*) they were very faithful and loyal citizens, who paid their taxes, were obedient to the Emperor in every other matters; and were willing to provide any other service the Emperor may demand in the extension and maintenance of the civil order and good government.

The Yehudes on the other hand had already produced literature in defence of their Faith and practice–*Wisdom of Solomon*; Philo wrote a treatise *On Contemplative Life*: Flavius Josephus wrote: *Against Apion, 2vv* circa 70; *Jewish Antiquities* circa 80; *Jewish Wars*. circa 90.

Among the Christians, perhaps Luke on Paul's address at Athens (*Acts 17. 22-31*) counted. The earliest booklet was *Preaching of Peter* which was later quoted in Clement of Alexandria and Origen. Heracleon, a pupil of Valentinus wrote commentaries on Luke and John's gospels *circa* AD170–180 from Rome.

- Production of Christian Literature for believers and in defence of Christianity

Aristides the Christian philosopher of Athens

Aristides wrote *Apology of Aristides* c. AD 138 – AD 147 and *The Gospel of Hebrews* from Egypt. Eusebius accepted *First Epistle of Peter* as Petrine writing. But the *Acts of Peter, The Gospel of Peter* and *The Revelation of Peter* were not treated as Petrine writings. Aristobulus of Pella (*in Perea*) wrote about the times of the siege of Jerusalem (AD68-AD70) by Titus, the son of Emperor Vespasian. His warning was "escape to Pella." Those who took his warning escaped annihilation. Lord Jesus also recommended Pella! Justin Martyr tried allegory (c. AD110) to convince the Yehudes that Jesus was the predicted and long awaited *Sage* in his *Dialogue with Trypo*. Justin was an inveterate apologist. He was on to attacking Marcion (c. AD85–c.AD140s), the son of a bishop and a prosperous shipping magnate of Sinope in Pontus. Marcion was a generous donor to good causes. The early Christians had not yet a fully developed Christian writings. (*i.e., a canonical compendium*) Individual letters and commentaries were hand written and were circulating and read aloud at worship services in many emerging congregations.

Marcion pleaded for usage of contemporary writings of Jesus era but plea went unheeded

Marcion was perhaps a very thoughtful person with an analytical mind. He looked at the Yehudic texts still being used by the early followers of the Lord. Marcion felt that the whole codified Yehudic Laws were incongruent with Lord Jesus teachings of mercy, love and compassion. Consequently, he wrote a critical tome *Contradictions* and wished that the public readings at church be limited to contemporary Christian books–the Gospel of Luke and the ten letters of Saul. He would have none of the blurring of the gross differences by the then popular allegorical approaches. He walked into a hornet nest. Justin of Rome was ready to tackle Marcion in his *Against all Heresies* and *Antithesis*. For sticking out his neck Justin was convicted of being a Christian and was martyred. Theophilus of Antioch was also opposed to Marcion. Marcion went to Rome to prevail upon the Western Christians to unify, with his version of limiting scriptures to post Jesus writings, but he was unsuccessful.

Irenaeus bishop and apologist

Irenaeus born in Asia Minor c.130–c.200 possibly met Polycarp, bishop of Smyrna. Irenaeus later became the bishop of Lyons in AD177. He was well versed in the theology and life-styles of both the Western and Eastern churches. He was into attacks against *Gnosticism*,

Montanism, and *Quarto-deciman* sectarian issues. Irenaeus vision and concern was the unity of the universal church, based on sound apostolic teachings. The apostles and those who learned from them were the ones to be trusted. The Roman church was one such institution which could be trusted. This was a boost to Eleutherus the then bishop of Rome (AD175-AD189). Irenaeus appealed to the Christian scriptures – the four gospels, Acts, the letters of Saul, the three pastoral letters to Timothy and Titus, 1 John, 1 Peter, Revelation of John and the Shepherd of Hermas, twenty two in all. Irenaeus was indebted to Justin's *Against Marcion* and he quoted from it.
(*Goodspeed pp.119-122*)

Hegesippus the Christian apologist and Roman writer

Hegesippus was a gentile Christian of Syria (*Goodspeed pp.123ff*) in his *Memoir* had argued that Marcion and Gnosticism were off-shoots of the seven Jewish sects of the times. His account of the martyrdom of James the brother of our Lord was very moving. Since James was well spoken of among the Jerusalem Jews, they asked him as their friend to denounce in public against the wildfire like spread of the Jesus Way taking place. The Jews led him to the highest location on the Temple mount to denounce Jesus and his followers.

When he spoke, he praised and honoured Lord Jesus. The mob was infuriated and stoned James to death and threw him down the cliff. He was still alive and prayed to God to forgive the persecutors for they were ignorant of what they were doing. A fuller who was nearby laundering used his fuller's rod to break the skull of James and he died. The crowd buried James at the very spot. (*Goodspeed p.124*)

[Eusebius *Church History* iii.20. 1-8 referred to the story of Hegesippus as occurring during the reign of Emperor

Domitian. In spite of the fact that the present author had a copy of Eusebius quotations found in Schaff vol. 1, 2nd series, 4th reprint 2004 of the original 1890 edition, he could not find such a citation!]

Clement of Alexandria

Clement (c. AD190 – AD215 in *Goodspeed pp. 130ff*) in his *Outlines* claimed that the letter to the Hebrews was written by Saul. Clementine writings were lost over the centuries like many other writings of the early period. Clement also wrote about the pathos of the current Greek values and life-styles as if to prepare them for the message of Lord Jesus. (*Goodspeed p.129*) Clementine scriptures included the letter to Hebrews, 1 Clement, Barnabas, the Shepherd of Hermas, Revelation of Peter, preaching of Peter and the Teachings of the Twelve Apostles. He knew of the gospel of Hebrews and the gospel of Egyptians and the traditions of Matthias. He did not accept them as scriptures but he did not dismiss them as heretical either. (*Goodspeed p.133*)

Origen of Alexandria

Origen was a native of Alexandria. (c. *AD184–AD269*)

He was so learned that at 18 was made the head of the Catechetical School by Bishop Demetrius. He continued for 12 years in this position. He was a prolific writer. The Roman Emperor went on an attack, hence Origen got out to Caesarea for two years. He often preached at the request of the bishops of Jerusalem and Caesarea. When he returned to Alexandria he managed to teach, write and preach for 13 more years. He also revisited Athens and Arabia. Emperor Maximin AD 235 – AD 238 drove Origen out to Caesarea in Cappodocia. In the Deciman persecution Origen was imprisoned and suffered physical tortures and died in AD

254 at age 69. Ambrose, a wealthy man supported Origen in his publishing work. (*Goodspeed. pp.132–135*)

Hippolytus of Alexandria

Hippolytus described the Church order in Alexandria (*Coptic Church*). It gave direction on ordination of bishops, presbyters and deacons, the prayers to be offered and on confessors, widows, virgins, new converts, crafts forbidden to Christians, on baptism, confirmation, observances, fasts and prayers in concise and practical manner, a great codifier. His *Manual* goes back to AD 215. His canon contained the four gospels, 13 letters of Paul, but not Hebrews. He accepted Acts, three catholic letters 1 Peter, 1 John, 2 John, and Revelation. (25). With Hippolytus ends Greek Christianity in Rome due to the rise of Latin. He was a moral purist. He made substantial contribution to Christian development. (*Goodspeed pp. 149,150*)

Chapter 31

LATIN CHRISTIANITY

Tertullianus of Carthage

Tertullianus in North Africa, in the last part of the first Century of our era became active in Latin Christianity. Quintius Septimus Tertullianus was born in Carthage *circa*. AD 150–AD 160. He had knowledge of Athens and Rome in early life, while studying law. At Rome he also practiced Law and taught rhetoric with much success. He got converted to the Christian faith in Rome and returned to Carthage. Ambrose thought that Tertullianus on return to Carthage became a presbyter. He was a gifted writer and active in Church affairs during persecutions. He wrote much and was prepared for martyrdom under Emperor Commodus in AD 180. Seven men and five women suffered martyrdom in Carthage in a neighbouring town of Scilly. Tertullian in his *To the Heathen–Ad Nationes 2vv* AD 197 protested much against laws condemning Christians as such. He fought back the charges of incest, child murder and disloyalty to the Empire. He countered earlier ways of exposing undesired children among the pagan.

Cyprian of Carthage

Cyprian was another Latin priest from North Africa was made a bishop by popular demand only two years after his conversion to Christianity. Cornelius was the bishop of Rome during this time, after the Emperor Decius persecution. (*AD253 – AD260*) Cyprian was vigorous in his concern for unity of the Church which had to be achieved in the unity of the bishops. He reluctantly agreed to support Cornelius Bishop of Rome in his desire for the recognition of the See of Rome as the most important See, hence a superior status.

Under the persecution of Emperor Valerian (AD253–AD260), Cyprian was banished from the bishopric of Carthage in AD257 to Curubis 40 miles away. He just moved to the new location and continued his work of propagation of the gospel. Cyprian was arrested and beheaded in September AD258. Decius introduced new laws of persecution based on circumstances. The penalty for clergy was death; for other leaders, varying degrees of punishment–confiscation of property, degradation and even slavery.

At the request of Quirinius the procurator, Cyprian codified the Christian religious texts then available–the four gospels, Acts, 13 letters of Saul, 1 Peter, 1 John and the book of Revelation. He did not include the letter to Hebrews. (*Goodspeed p.171*)

Lactantius the scholar, writer

Lactantius (c. AD250 – c. AD325) was a pupil of Arnobius in North Africa. He wrote much and Emperor Constantine asked him to leave for Treves in Gaul to tutor his ten years old son Crispus. His writings were voluminous. His *Divine Institutes* was larger than the present New Testament. He also wrote *On False Religions, On the Origin of Error, On False Wisdom, On True Wisdom, On Justice, On True Worship,*

On the Happy Life. It appears they were revised in AD 313. Lactantius added three more volumes – *On the Wrath of God, On the Deaths of Persecutors, Epitome of the Institutes* in AD 314. One assumes the persecuting emperors were Nero, Domitian, Decius, Valerian and Aurelius. Lactantius also described the then current persecutors–Diocletian, Maximus, Galerius and Maximin. Later, Hi writings were read much by Jerome of Rome and Augustine of Hippo.

Organizational Need

On the necessity for organization, one turns to J. W. C. Wand *A History of the Early Church to AD500*. Methuen, London, 3rd ed. 1949. Wand has argued that Lord Jesus himself had organized a faithful group. Such an organization was to be securely founded 'on a rock.' The initiation was by baptism and the authority of the Lord and his apostolic leadership would ensure its care for the moral wellbeing of its members; and the special favour of God would be granted to its united intercessions. Jesus himself had already chosen and trained the leaders. The social element was fundamental. It was an ever widening circle from Galilee to Rome (*Wand pp 2 and 3*).

One learns of the Jerusalem Pharisee Sect, which was vehemently opposed to the Maccabean Hellenizing efforts. All the same even the Pharisees had absorbed much of the Persian dualism, spiritism and eschatology. The high priesthood was part of the Sadducee group which had long been subject to the pagan political influence, hence Hellenism found strong support from them. Wand also reminded us, of the rabbis or teachers who were opposed to the Helenization process. They were opposed to the continuation of the Roman rule. From time to time Rome intervened and quashed opposition movements e.g., the Zealots. The Roman garrison in Jerusalem kept a watchful eye on rebels. Roman power was at its zenith–Carlisle to Nile. One coinage, one language would carry the traveller everywhere.

Wand highlighted the slow erosion of moral and spiritual values in the far extended empire. The households accepted many gods for diverse purposes. Christianity appealed to one divinity which was challenging to the deprived masses. Some of the emperors assumed for themselves the status of divinity. (*Wand pp. 9–12*)

In the face of continuous rebellion, Gessius Florus the procurator of Judaea put to death over 3,000 Jews in AD66. The Jews revolted. To resolve the problem, as a final solution, Titus son of Vespasian was sent and the move resulted in the total destruction of Jerusalem and its temple. The Christian residents discretely moved out to Pella and escaped annihilation.

Wand brought out the problems of conversion of marital-partners to the new Faith. If one got converted and the other did not there was possibility for tensions and possible breakup of relationships. This has been problematic ever since. Enthusiasm for proselytising people of other Faiths often did not result in harmonious transition. Often there were also economic and emotional repercussions among the kinsfolk. However, there were very few instances of kinsfolk suffering because of conversions due to evangelism. (*Wand pp.15, 16*)

We learn from Wand of the internal struggles among the followers of the apostles. There were the Petrine and Pauline parties. It had become a major issue for a time. Saul was an aggressive 'go-getter,' while Peter was not given to aggressive recruitment. It was the followers who felt aggrieved and formed parties in support of one or the other of the two apostles.

Some explanation for the development of *Gnosticism* is needed. Christians were allowed to become members of elite pagan clubs. There emerged intermingling and ideological compromises. It may account for the development of Gnosticism. Ebionites were a Yehudic sect which rejected the divine sonship of Jesus, while accepting him as messiah, the greatest prophet. There were then Pharisees and Ebionites; and a third faction was Docetic. Docetism saw Jesus as truly God but his appearance as Jesus in flesh and blood was phantasmal. It was against such a view that the Johanine gospel and epistles were written.

Christianity, according to Wand contained elements from all three of the above mentioned sects. Wand considered emphasis on unity and authority of the elders as central to the survival of the new community of the Lord's followers. Peace of God had to be important for any serious attempts at unity and authority. (*Wand pp. 21-23*)

Didache: The Teachings of the Twelve Apostles

Didache probably originated in Antioch towards the end of the first century. It was another early document. The challenge provided in *Didache* was contrasting two ways, the way to death and the way to life. It was a primitive church's penitential system that one did not attend the prayer services without confession of wrongful conscience to the church . It was also about asceticism. It maintained that if one could bear the yoke (*ascetic practice*) of the Lord, one could become perfect. If one was unable to bear the yoke of the Lord one may try what one could manage. (*Wand pp 24-26*)

Wand referred to Harnach who believed that on the basis of 1 Corinthian 12. 28f and Ephesians 4.11f, it could be claimed that the ministry of preaching and ministry of administration were distinctly separate. The ministry of preaching was carried out by the apostles, prophets and teachers. This was a gift from God, hence called charismatic ministry of universal significance. They travelled from one community to another. The ministry of administration was a human appointment, namely bishops and deacons. Wand noted that such clear distinction were not of relevance for the Church which spread like wild fire within the first century itself. The concerns raised in *Didache* were to do with the transition period in which the local congregation was beginning to adapt to 'functions and authority' of the charismatic ministry. The need for unity and the maintenance of authority were of primary significance. (*Wand pp 28, 29*)

The apostles stayed put in Jerusalem even after the day of Pentecost and often met for prayer and worship at the temple as witnessed in the healing of the lame man at the temple entrance. As mentioned earlier, the apostles worshipped at the temple at Jerusalem or attended a synagogue close to wherever they travelled. Wand had claimed that the organizational pattern of the new religion was not borrowed from Greek sources but Jewish sources.

The present author was not convinced that the Greeks and Romans did not provide models for the social and faith organizations of both Yehudism and for the Christian Church. Rome ruled Judaea, including Galilee, Samaria and Syria. The Roman organizational structure and process indeed had a powerful role in the life-style of the conquered. In India the British left their mark on the organizational structure of the Republic of India and the Islamic Republic of Pakistan.

Emperor Hadrianus

Emperor Hadrianus (*AD 117–AD 138*) was tired of continual wars and rebellions in the far flung empire. He tried to seek after peace by playing fair to the conquered nations. (*Wand pp.30-32*) Bar Cochba of the Yehudes tried one more time to rebel in AD 132. With great difficulty but with equally great severity Hadrianus crushed the rebellion and completely destroyed everything Yehudic and in the place of the Jerusalem temple a Roman temple was built Aelia Capitolina which did not permit Yehudes to enter, on pain of death. Muncius Fundanus was appointed as the new pro-consul of Asia. Anonymous accusations were not tolerated. Eighty six years old Polycarp, the bishop of Smyrna was burnt alive. The Yehudes who were hateful of the Christians, even in the face of their own persecutions, still gloated over the murder of Bishop Polycarp. (*Wand p.37*)

Apologist writings during a lull in persecution

During a lull in persecution, in the first half of second century, apologists wrote their missives for toleration, the first of which was already mentioned, Justin Martyr. The apologists concern was to explain their position. The Christians were good citizens and obeyed the Emperor and were loyal, even though they did not offer worship to the emperor. These were open letters. It was doubtful if the emperors ever read any of them. The emperors had enough on hand to be reading philosophical treatises with fine rhetoric. The aim of the apologist was to inform the Roman intelligentsia of the innocence and good citizenship of the Christians. Apologetics took diverse forms. One was open letters addressed to the Emperor, but read by the public rather than the emperor *per se*. The second format was to the public-at-large. (e.g., *Address to the Greeks*). A third approach was to address high ranking individuals. They were fighting on two fronts, one to defend the new belief system of the Christians; and then to show that their new found faith was far superior to anything that existed then. Some of the apologies were focussed on the pagan and others on the Yehudes. (*Wand p.37*)

Philip Schaff and History of Christianity to end of 19th Century

In the late Nineteenth Century, Philip Schaff in his *History of the Christian Church* series, focussed on *Apostolic Christianity: From Birth of Christ to the Death of St John* in his Volume 1. Schaff provided an exhaustive survey of the period. He too considered the Pharisees as traditionalists and fanatically orthodox. In fact, the Jerusalem Jews of the non-Hellenist background fitted the description. John the Baptist, Elizabeth, Mary and Our Lord Jesus were their targets as they most likely were of Hellenist heritage.

The Jewish women and children benefitted from pharisaic clearly defined dogma and instructions from the teachers of religious laws. They sustained the pattern of behavioural norms and their alleged moral significance. Jesus called them 'hypocrites' as they were very self-righteous (*Schaff p.64*)

As stated earlier, the Sadducees were from fairly well-off classes who had control over cash.

The finances and the treasury were under their domain. Unlike the Pharisees, the Sadducees accepted the reality of Roman suzerainty. They were sceptics and rationalists who knew how to manipulate the Roman authority to their advantage. They got along with the Roman governors and procurators. They were 'embedded.' They accepted the Pentateuch but rejected the oral traditions when it suited them. Over against the radical young *Rebe* Jesus, they could collude with the Pharisees. They were not impressed by concepts like life after death or immortality of the 'soul.' Indeed historically, most Yehudic understanding tended to be this worldly. Persian 'dualism' was a later innovation assimilated during the exile and irrelevant for them. (*Schaff p.65*)

The Essenes of the north-east Africa truly relied on the Yehudic proclivity to hope of the future as the Egyptian arid desert suited doing their own thing of extreme asceticism.

The present author's focus is limited to the first century spread of Jesus Way, while the Alexandrian Christians (*Coptic*) were of the second and third centuries.

To the Romans, the present and past mattered; however when tempted with divine status, some of the Emperors were not averse to notions of future dynasty. Theoretically, to the Yehudes and Christians, the future was considered as of 'paramount' importance. However, when it came to practice, our greed for power, possession, prestige and propaganda values really mattered. If life-styles are indicators, then our greed for material possessions indeed became of paramount importance After making such a drastic criticism, it must also be stated that it was the Christians who excel in personal and material support for the needy during natural calamities around the globe.

As stated before, the Yehudes owed much to Consul Pompeii for his settling many Yehudes on the banks of Tiber, when he took many prisoners from Judaea as he conquered the whole area including Jerusalem in BC 63. The talented Yehudes from among the prisoners thrived in Rome. Soon they became merchants and influential people and claimed *religio licita* status.

Christians began to gain ground in Rome through the missionary efforts of Peter; and later Saul had his followers established themselves in Rome. However, the Christians were still not wealthy enough to claim any status. Their religion was *religio-illicita,* hence persecuting them was fair game and not unconscionable.

The Roman Empire was colossal in it spread from the Euphrates to the Atlantic, from the Libyan desert to the banks of the Rhine, whose population was estimated around 100 million. It was claimed that the Yehudes who were settled in Rome were thriving well that there were seven Yehudic synagogues and three cemeteries in Rome by the time of Peter and Saul in AD 66. The Yehude merchants and their kinsfolk spread out all over the world, according to Josephus and Strabo. The Jewish communities made up part of the population of many cities. Josephus enjoyed favour of the Emperors Vespasian, Titus and Domitian.

Jerusalem Yehudism and the temple tax

Titus made sure that the temple of Jerusalem was completely destroyed. One of the problems which the Yehudes faced was that when the Jerusalem temple was annihilated, the Yehudes still had to pay temple taxes and the temple taxes were sent for the maintenance of the new Roman temple to Jupiter Capitolina which irritated the Yehudes to no end. All the smart young men were sent to Rome to be tutored in Latin ways. The Jerusalem Yehudic life-styles were a losing proposition under the Latin influence.

However, the Yehudes would try to maintain their old life-styles, hence the continued struggle between the Jerusalem and the Palestinian Yehudes and the Graeco-Latin Yehude turned Christians. Many of the Greek and other pagan converts to Yehudism resisted submission to the rite of circumcision. They were glad to join the Christians who only required of their converts to avoid idolatry, food sacrificed at the idolatrous worship and to avoid sexual immorality. Many of the converts were very liberal compared to their Jerusalem and Palestinian counterparts. The Church of Antioch became popular with such liberal converts. The fairly liberal minded Barnabas and Saul a strict Pharisee turned Christian were the leaders at Antioch. Furthermore, Christianity found a real foothold among the Samaritans.

Some of the writings of the Sub-Apostolic Era (AD1- AD100)

The powerful preaching and mass conversions attributed to Stephen, Philip and Peter prior to the Pentecost was the beginnings of propagation of the good news of the coming of God in human flesh, soul and spirit. The Sub-Apostolic Era as defined was the period AD1 *(approximating the birth of Lord Jesus)* to the end of the ministry of John the apostle who died around AD98 and extended to AD100 to AD110, the era of Justin Martyr.

We owed it to the Yehudic historian Flavius Josephus and the pagan historian Claudius Tacitus, two thorough going haters of the followers of Jesus Way for material on the persecutions of Nero, the Roman Emperor the latest by AD66. The chief of the apostles Peter was crucified upside down on the Vatican Hill and buried there. Saul was beheaded and buried on the Ostian Way at the three hills outside the city of Rome.

The writings of Peter and Saul could only have taken place between AD37 and AD66, if indeed they wrote them. It was most likely that the devout disciples of the apostles may later have committed to writing what were originally the homilies at community gatherings and notes taken down of the answers to questions posed by the hearers of the preaching of the apostles and apostolic leaders. Peter emphasized the primary importance of conversion and faith in Jesus as the only Name whereby any one could attain eternal life. The converts were vibrant and displayed a sense of joy and triumph. This experience has been true of most converts throughout the history of Christianity.

The preaching of Saul was focused on the Gentiles and he used Greek philosophy and logic to bring out the truths of the teachings of Lord Jesus. Saul tried to link Jesus teachings with the Yehudic Laws as 'fulfillment' of the ancient Yehudic law-giver's alleged 'predictions' for the future. Alas, as mentioned earlier, the Church got sucked into this scheme to its detriment. The powerful message of 'God becoming human as 'incarnation' was somewhat sidelined and 'Jesus Way' was seen as fulfilment of Yehudic Laws!

John survived severe persecution in a miraculous way and was able to tell the stories of the early growth of the Church till his death in AD98. The Apocalypse was probably written in AD 68, 69. The Gospel and the epistles were written by John in mid-nineties. John was busy either presiding at the dedication or establishment of churches in towns and villages or, confirming converts. The communities sought John's advice all the time.

The Martyrdom of James the Just

James, the brother of Jesus was a leader of the Jerusalem Church. He was trying to provide a bridge between the newly emerging and fast spreading Jesus Way and the Yehudic Christians of Jerusalem who saw Jesus as 'Messiah' and scrupulously practised the ritual laws of the old order. The Jerusalem Jews panicked, when they realized how fast and how widespread was the Christian outreach. They pleaded with James to speak out against the wildfire like spread of the Jesus Way.

The Pharisees placed James on the pinnacle of the Temple and asked him to denounce Jesus. James shouted aloud that Jesus was indeed risen after crucifixion, death and burial and ascended to heaven and would return soon to reward his believers. The mob was enraged and threw James down and beat him to death with a fuller's rod. All the same, some of those who had heard James believed and became followers of Jesus. It was ironic that the next day Emperor Vespasian invaded Judea, according to Josephus' *Antiquities*. (*Schaff pp 276, 277*)

Peter and John leaders at Antioch in Syria

Peter and John laid the foundation of Gentile Christianity at Antioch in Syria before the new convert Saul became a prominent voice at Antioch. As mentioned earlier, the Elder Barnabas, a wealthy man from Cyprus took Saul under his wings and initiated him into missionary work. Saul may have been an impetuous person, who always wished to be the leader both in behaviour and in articulation of advice, rebuke or exhortation. He also had a tendency to get things done. These characteristics may have been a result of his diminutive personality with some physical debility added to it.

It was noted that Saul was short and heavily bearded and a bald head and not a physically attractive personality. However, he could be a charmer as well. He was likely to enjoy people surround him and look up to him. Indeed there were a few who really looked up to him. He used his two imprisonment travails, to pen epistles to his Christian friends and converts in various important towns and cities of the Roman world. (*Schaff pp. 278, 279*).

A time came when Saul parted company from Barnabas the Elder and went on his own to revisit some of the congregations which emerged as a result of their preaching efforts. Barnabas accompanied by John Mark went on another evangelistic tour. John Mark was a fairly well-off businessman who had to attend to his mother's business after his return from the first evangelistic trip with Saul. These facts were stat3ed earlier on. There may be other factors at work too. Saul was a difficult person to work with if one reads between the lines!

If we turn to a later history, we learn that in the face of expectations of persecutions, some followers of the Lord decided on celibate life-style. *The Acts of Paul and Thecla* would encourage celibacy in the second and third centuries. Clement of Rome, writing in the early second century informed that there were written attacks against Saul. Some disciples and followers of Peter were saddened by Saul's attracting disciples away from Peter and they wrote supportive of Peter.

Whatever be the differences, which may have emerged during their tireless missionary work, Peter and Saul were together in Rome at the time of their martyrdom in AD66. The Roman bishops claimed that their apostle was Peter who established the Church in Rome and was their bishop for 25 years. All the same, Peter was often on travels, even though he was recognized as the bishop of Rome by later historians. This tradition of Peter's leadership in Rome withstood the test of time to this day.

It needs to be emphasized that the Christianization of the Roman citizenry was begun through the apostolic teams visiting the Jewish settlements and entering their synagogues and availing themselves of the opportunities provided for addressing the congregation. There were subtle signs of discrimination against the 'outsiders' at such assemblies. The Greek and other fairly well off pagan friends of the local Yehudic communities which were spread all over the Mediterranean were attracted to the Christian message and in short order a sizeable population of the urban, suburban and rural folks accepted the morally sound religion and ethics of the followers of Lord Jesus; and by the end of the first century they were found everywhere. See the attached map from Ronald Brownrigg. *The Twelve Apostles*.

Chapter 32

A BRIEF NOTE ON ACTIVITIES OF THE TWELVE APOSTLES AND EPILOGUE AND PROGNOSIS

St Andrew: was from Bethsaida living at Capernaum. He preached the gospel among the primitive people of Scythia, the wild stepplands beyond the Carpathians and the Caucasus, the territory to the north-east of the Roman Empire. Today, it is part of south Russia, beyond Danube and north of the Black Sea. In these areas there were no Yehudic communities. It is also possible, Andrew was ministering in Greece. He may have journeyed to Macedonia, Byzantium, Thrace, Perinthus, Philippi and Thessalonica. He was possibly martyred for converting Maximilla the wife of Aegeates, pro-consul of Achaia out of jealousy. St Andrew was a creative person who had achieved much for the spread of the gospel.

St. Bartholomew: son of Talmai, a friend of Philip. He could be Nathaniel. Names were interchangeable. He was both an apostle and deacon. Polycarp, bishop of Smyrna, affirmed that he was an apostle. The apocryphal *Acts of Philip* of the fourth century link the two together. There was a distinct tradition linking Bartholomew to his travels to Armenia and possibly to northwest of India. Philip's sister Mariamne was a friend of Bartholomew who had visited Hierapolis with Stachys. He was also at Lycaonia. He was martyred by being hung naked. There was a gospel of Bartholomew mentioned by Jerome in the early fourth century. There was an apocryphal anecdote on Bartholomew conversing with Jesus about the Lord's descent from the cross and visiting the nether world to bring out Adam the first man and all Patriarchs, Abraham, Issac and Jacob. It was alleged that Bartholomew had asked Jesus as to which were the sins against the Holy Spirit which could not be forgiven. It was claimed that Jesus had replied: 'hypocrisy and slander.' i.e., anyone who spoke against a person who served God with reverence. Jerome claimed that Bar Talmai was a descendent of Talmai whose daughter married King David. As a missionary to India, it was possible he had translated Christian writing. For all the traditions, it was most likely St. Bart was martyred in Armenia at Derbend. (*Brownrigg pp. 132–139*)

St James, Alphaeus: Known as James-the-less, possibly brother of Matthew ben Levi, brother of Jose son of Mary. John Chrysostom of the fourth century considered that both Matthew and James were involved in customs duties, brother publicans, who were collectors of public revenue, which was hated by the poorer segments of the Yehudic society. It is very likely that they were cousins of Lord Jesus. James appeared under three different names – Alphaeus, Clopas and Cleopas, brother of Joseph the carpenter of Nazareth.

St James ben Zebadee: Older brother of John and a cousin of Lord Jesus; and fisherman of Capernaum. He was the first martyr in AD44, by Herod Antipas the Jerusalem high priest and interim procurator of Judaea while waiting for a replacement from Rome. He was present at the post resurrection appearances of our Lord.

St. John ben Zebadee: Younger brother to James and the youngest and favourite disciple of Lord Jesus. He outlived all the apostles till AD98 and was the protector of Mary the mother of Lord Jesus. He had high level connections with the Jerusalem Yehudic hierarchy. His gospel was all about symbols and themes for Christian life-style. The two brothers were sons of Salome. They had some means and owned a sizable sailing vessel for deep sea fishing and employed hired crew. The father and mother were skilled in business and finance. Salome may have provided Jesus with some financial support for his ministry.

St. Matthew ben Levi: He was also referred to as son of Alphaeus. Anne his spouse was sister of Mary the mother of Lord Jesus and probably lived in Bethsaida. The Father was a fisherman. He was despised as was his brother for serving the Roman government as customs collectors. The customs and tax collectors were bonded together to support one another. In Latin, the customs collector role was described '*publicani*.' Jesus had invited himself to their home. Lord Jesus called Matthew and James to follow him and they did without any hesitancy.

St. Peter: Perhaps Peter was the oldest apostle of Lord Jesus. He was also the chief apostle of the Lord. He lived in Bethsaida on the lake Galilee. There were ten major cities around the lake for fishing and export import business. Through Galilee ran the ancient trade route between Egypt and Mesopotamia; Syria and Greece. The Yehudes were a business community surrounded by non-Yehudes of considerable number. The Roman Christian community considered Peter as their leader. Rome was the capital of the Roman Empire. The religious headquarter of the Christian Church must also be located there, ran the argument. It was a strategic decision and it proved to be a wise judgement for the times. The great basilica of Peter was built over Peter's tomb. The epistles of Peter were written in a refined Greek and style, hence it is thought, Mark his amanuensis put together the homilies of Peter into a compendium of Peter's teachings as his epistles. 1 Peter circulated from ancient times. It was Peter the chief disciple who made history and not the writings *per se*. He was the Lord's chosen leader after him. From Pentecost onwards, it was Peter who was the unchallenged leader. Peter was a persuasive preacher and the Holy Spirit honoured his efforts. (*Brownrigg pp. 41-47*)

St Philip: Historically, Philip's story was tied with that of St Bartholomew. They were provisioner for the needy. Philip had two daughters and they were prophets. He was a successful evangelist. He was a spirit filled man. He helped a treasurer of the Ethiopian Queen who was a 'God-fearer' become a Christian. Philip baptized him at his request. Philip was found introducing people to Lord Jesus. He could debate with 300 rhetoricians and still win. It was possible that Philip was of high standing and influence at Caesarea. He healed the sick and raised to life a young boy. He preached as far as Lydia and Asia Minor. One of the converts of Philip was Nicanora the Jewish wife of the Roman pro-consul. The pro-consul out of jealousy hung Philip to death. It is possible that Philip established a congregation at Athens and ordained a bishop and presbyter and departed to Parthia to preach. Eusebius considered him 'Great light of Asia.' (*Brownrigg pp.129-133*)

St Simon the eager one: One of the four nationalistic disciples was Simon the Zealot. Even with such a background, Simon and the other three kept faith with Jesus through crucifixion, resurrection and ascension. He was present with the 120 at Pentecost and carried the message of love to the Gentile world. Simon and Thaddaeus worked as a team and spent 13 years preaching throughout the 12 provinces of the Persian Empire (eastern provinces) and saw 60,000 people become followers of the Lord in Babylon. Simon and Judas

Thaddaeus were stoned to death. But the gospel spread all the same. [It has been suggested that part of the Persian Empire was occupied by the Yehudic people during the fourth century BC through the 11th century AD]. It became problematic to understand what was meant by the 'Babylonian captivity.' It was possible that there were misunderstandings of the residential movement or location *per se*. Simon was martyred.

St Thaddaeus: The story of Thaddaeus was same as that of Simon the eager one. They worked as a team. After the last supper, Thaddaeus exclaimed why the rest of the Jewish world could not be convinced of the Messiahship of Jesus. He challenged Jesus for a public demonstration of his power. Jesus expressed that men's heart must be won for the Father and him (Jesus) to dwell in them. Brownrigg had suggested that Judas son of James could be identified as Thaddaeus. It was possible that his friends had nicknamed him as 'Busty Judas' to distinguish him from the 'traitor Judas.' He was also a Zealot commando or dagger-man. The dagger was a short curved one (*sicarius in Latin*) carried at the waist, possibly similar to the one found among the Kurds and Sikhs. The *Sicarii* developed as a guerrilla group within the patriotic Zealot party. They were pledged to expel the Romans by violence, assassination and terrorism, if necessary. Thus, it could be adduced that both the father and son as fanatics and nationalistic in the hopes of liberation of the Jewish people from the dominance of Rome. They expected Jesus would have fulfilled their hope. Thaddaeus was martyred. (*Brownrigg pp.161,163,175,201*)

St Thomas (Didymus): This 'doubting' Thomas was a great missionary traveller and established churches in Parthia and India. He was a courageous man. Jerome confirmed that Thomas journeyed to India via the Red-Sea route. Thomas probably landed at Muziris (Kodungalore in Kerala). It was possible that the Raja of the times may have invited Thomas who was a carpenter architect. He was also in Mylapore (*Chennai*) on the east coast. In modern times a huge Gothic Church was built (*1896*) on the alleged spot where Thomas was daggered to death. Roman coins of the times of emperors Tiberius and Caligula were found in Bangalore.

Judas Iscariot: The story of a financial expert Iscariot, the self appointed Treasurer of the Jesus team was a marred one, as he not only pilfered some of the money given to Jesus cause, but out of his misjudged zeal to encourage the Lord to take action to become the king. Having failed in his persuasiveness, he had committed suicide. The Lord Jesus knew of what Judas Iscariot would do and yet permitted him to be a follower and be one of the twelve disciples. The story of Judas Iscariot has been visited and re-visited by scholars and preachers. One thing was certain. Judas Iscariot was one of the many Jewish nationalists who were very desperate in their quest for the overthrow of the Roman yoke. One wonders whether Judas Iscariot's pilfering was basically to support the nationalist cause and he was, according to the gospel accounts let down by the Yehudic leadership. Lord Jesus was acutely aware of the zeal of His disciples and He was not necessarily worried about the overthrow of the Roman yoke *per se*, but relative to the given situation, His focus was the redemption of the soul/spirit from the inner oppressions, towards eternal life, the life beyond the earthly sphere.

Epilogue and Prognosis

Given the circumstances of the author vis-à-vis, access to academic Libraries, he has attempted to explore the possible outworking of the universal message of Lord Jesus, Son of God who walked the earth two thousand years ago. Jesus had clearly instructed his apostles to stay-put in Jerusalem and wait for the out-pouring of the Holy Spirit on the day of

Pentecost to be energized for the spread of the mission He himself had initiated in Galilee, Judaea and Samaria.

The apostles, devout women and men numbering about 120 were to be endued with power from the gift of the Holy Spirit before they launched on their mission first to the Jerusalem Yehudes, thence to the Hellenists and the Samaritans and on to the peoples all over the known world of the Roman Empire and beyond. Jesus had set up a model of an organizational structure for the apostles to follow.

Jesus had taught the apostles by his own example of preaching, teaching, healing and organizing communities for the future spread of the good news that God had manifested Himself in Jesus, out of His mercy and compassion for the despised and the outcasts. God was love incarnate in Jesus.

The author tried to account for the ministry of the apostolic community during the first century which was a difficult era for the followers of the Lord. Praises be to God, the message of the blessed Incarnate One spread like wild-fire in much of the Roman Empire in a matter of a few decades creating jealousy of the Yehudic and pagan mini-leaders of the Empire. The number of converts may not be in the tens of thousands, but the scope of the out-reach area of the Roman Empire and beyond was indeed staggering.

It is up to the present day followers of Lord Jesus to continue to serve in genuine compassion and a spirit of self-giving service to every community all over the world, especially those who desperately need or, quest for eternal life; and healthcare, fresh water, grain and vegetables for their sustenance and freedom from emotional and physical oppressions. Where the gospel was preached there the comprehensive needs of the people of all walks of life were also attended to. "This is our story, this is our song, praising our Saviour all the day long."

DAILY PRAYERS

Morning Prayer

Opening sentences:
O God! Creation's secret force, yourself Unmoved, all motion's source! From dawn till dusk, through all its changes guide us this day (*based on St. Ambrose*)
"More than anything else put God's work first; do what He wants" (*Mt. 6.33*)
The Lord is not slow about keeping his promises. God is patient, because he wants everyone to turn from errors and no one to be lost. (*Based on 2 Peter 3: 9*)

Penitence and Confession:

Most Merciful and Compassionate Lord! Hear us and enable us to lead a life this day, as we enter upon our daily tasks. Grant us penitence and accept our humble entreaties and forgive us; grant us spiritual, emotional and strength of will to fulfil all our daily tasks worthy of the Blessed Lord Jesus, *Amen*.

Absolution: The Most Merciful God, for the sake of the Incarnate Lord Jesus grants us the grace and forgiveness; and the awareness of the presence of the Holy Spirit in our lives towards truth, justice, and hope of life to come for ages and ages. *Amen*

Proclamation of the Word:
Jesus Parable: A man had a guest arrived at mid-night for whom he had nothing to offer. He approaches his old friend to borrow some food. Jesus said, even though it was late, the man would still get up and give as much as his friend needed. Jesus went on: "Ask and you will receive; search and you will find; knock and the door will be opened for you." "Which one of you fathers would give your child a snake if he asks for a fish? As bad as you are, you still know how to give good gifts to your children. But your heavenly father is even more ready to give the Holy Spirit to anyone who asks."

Creed:
We are not alone; we live in God's world. We believe in God, who has created and is creating; who has come in Jesus, the Incarnate one made flesh, to reconcile and make new, who works in us and others by the Spirit. We trust in God. We are called to be the Church: to celebrate God's presence, to live with respect in creation, to love and serve others, to seek justice and resist evil, to proclaim Jesus, crucified and Risen, our judge and our hope. In life and death, in life beyond death, God is with us. We are not alone. Thanks be to God*!*

Intercession and Thanksgiving: Here offer intercessions for: The Apostolic Church (*Roman, Orthodox and Protestant Churches- Lutheran, Reformed, Anglican, Baptist, Pentecostal and other* churches) all in authority; needs of world; sharing and not greed; local community; for people in need; for repose of the souls of departed. Thanksgiving.

Lord's Prayer   **Dismissal:** Let us bless the Lord! Thanks be to God! Amen

Daily Prayers

Noon Day Prayer

O God! Hear our prayers and Thanksgivings for the noon hour!

Jesus said: "And I, if I be lifted up, will draw all people to me."

Glory be to the Father, and to the Son and to the Holy Spirit: unto ages and ages, *Amen*.

Father of mercies, who to your Apostle Peter did reveal in three-fold vision your boundless compassion: forgive, we pray our unbelief, and so enlarge our hearts, and enkindle our zeal, that we may fervently desire the spiritual well being of all people and be more ready in due diligence and labour in the extension of your kingdom for the sake of the blessed Incarnate Lord Jesus. *Amen*.

The fruit of the Spirit is love, joy, peace, patience, kindness, goodness, faithfulness, gentleness, and self-control. If we live by the Spirit, let us also walk by the Spirit
(*based on Galatians 5: 22, 23a, 25*)

For whoever is in Jesus the Lord, there is a new creation; the past has gone, and the new one is here. It is all God's work. It was God who accepted us to Himself through Jesus, the Incarnate Lord and gave us the work of handing on this message of acceptance
(*based on 2 Corinthians 5: 17, 18*)

The Word of the Lord! Thanks Be to God!

Let us pray:

God! Have mercy; Incarnate Lord Jesus! Have mercy; God! Have mercy.

Heavenly Father! Send your Holy Spirit into our hearts to comfort us in all our concerns, responsibilities, and anxieties; and defend us from all error of judgement and lead us into all truth and trustworthiness through the Blessed Incarnate Lord Jesus. *Amen.*

Blessed Lord Jesus! At this hour you hung upon a cross, stretching out your loving arms. Grant that all our loved ones both far and near and our fellow citizens may look to you and be assured of your compassion and mercy. *Amen.*

The Lord's Prayer: Lord remember us in your kingdom, and teach us to pray:
Our Father who art in heaven, hallowed be thy name. Thy kingdom come; thy will be done on earth as in heaven. Give us this day our daily bread. Forgive us our wrong doings as we forgive those who have wronged against us. Save us from the times of trial, and deliver us from the evil one. For the kingdom, the power, and the glory are yours, to ages and ages, *Amen.*

Let us bless the Lord. Thanks be to God, *Amen!*

EVENING PRAYER

Jesus said: 'The time is coming and it is already here! Even now true worshipers are being led by the Spirit to worship the Father according to the truth. These are the ones the Father is seeking to worship him.' (*John 4: 23*)

Invitatory:

O Gracious Light, pure brightness of the everlasting Father in heaven, O Lord Jesus, holy and blessed*! Now* as we come to the setting of the sun and our eyes behold the dusk, we sing your praises, O! God! Father! Son and Holy Spirit! You are worthy at all times to be praised by happy voices! O Son of God, O Giver of life, and to be glorified through all the worlds! 'Be not afraid, only believe.' (*Bp Lee to Bp Westcott*)

We are not alone; we live in God's world. We believe in God: who has created and is creating, who has come in Jesus, the Incarnate one made flesh, to reconcile and make new, who works in us and others by the Spirit. We trust in God. We are called to be the Church: to celebrate God's presence, to live with respect in creation, to love and serve others, to seek justice and resist evil, to proclaim Jesus, crucified and Risen, our judge and our hope. In life and death, in life beyond death, God is with us. We are not alone. Thanks be to God.

Intercessions and Thanksgivings:

Let us pray: Offer intercessions for:-The Apostolic Church (*Roman; Orthodox and Protestant Churches–Lutheran; Baptist; Pentecostal; Anglican; and other Churches*)
-All in Authority; The needs of the wider world; sharing; the local community; people in especial need; for repose of the souls of the departed loved ones; General Thanksgiving.

The Lord's Prayer:

Following collects may also be said:

'O God from whom all holy desires, all good counsels, and all just works do proceed: Give to your servants that peace which the world cannot give; that our hearts may be set to obey your beloved Son's commandments; and also that by you we being defended from diverse kinds of fears, may pass our time in rest and quietness; through the merits of the Blessed Lord Jesus.' Amen

'Lighten our darkness, we beseech you O! Lord; and by your great mercy protect us from all perils and dangers of this night; for the love of your only Son, our Lord and Saviour Jesus.' Amen.

Benediction: The Grace of our Incarnate Lord Jesus and the love of God and the fellowship of the Holy Spirit be with us all, for evermore, *Amen!*

Compline (*Bed-time prayer*)

The Lord Almighty! Grant us a quiet night and a perfect end. *Amen*

Jesus said: 'If you are tired from carrying heavy burdens, come to me and I will give you rest....Take the yoke I give you. Put it on your shoulders and learn from me. I am gentle and humble, and you will find rest. This yoke is easy to bear, and this burden is light.' (*based on Matt 11: 28, 29, 30*).

Into your hands, O Lord we commend our spirit; for you have accepted us with all our failures and shortcomings, O Lord! You the God of truth! We commend our spirit.

Te lucis ante terminum

Before the ending of the day, Creator of the world, we pray
That with your, wonted favour you be, our guard and keeper now.

From all ill dreams defend our eyes; from nightly fears and fantasies;
Tread under foot our ghostly foe; that no pollution we may know.

O Father, that we ask be done; through Blessed Lord Jesus, your only Son;
Who, with the Holy Spirit and you, lives and reigns eternally. *Amen*

Keep us as the apple of an eye; hide us under the shadow of your wings.

Preserve us O Lord, waking: and guard us sleeping; that awake we may watch with Blessed Lord Jesus; and asleep we may rest in peace. *Amen!*

Lord Jesus! You are gentle with us as a mother with her children; and tenderly draw us from hatred and judgement. You comfort us in sorrow; and bind up our wounds. *Amen.* (*based on the Song of St. Anselm*)

Let us bless the Father, the Son, and the Holy Spirit; Let us praise him and magnify him forever. Vouchsafe Oh! Lord! To keep us this night without failures and shortcomings!
O Lord Jesus! Son of the living God, who at this evening hour did rest in the sepulchre, and did thereby sanctify the grave to be a bed of hope to your people: Make us so to abound in sorrow for our short-falls, which were the cause of your Passion, that wherein our bodies lie in the dust, our souls may live with thee; who lives and reigns with the Father and the Holy Spirit, one God, to ages and ages. *Amen.*

Be present, O merciful God and protect us through the silent hours of this night; that we, who are wearied by the changes and chances of this fleeting world, may repose upon your eternal changelessness. We will lay us down in peace and take our rest; for it is you Lord, who gives us rest; and makes us dwell in safety, *Amen*

The Lord's Prayer Let us bless the Lord! Thanks be to God!

BIBLIOGRAPHY

Appavoo, Muthiah David *Yesu Avtar*: Teachings and Stories of Blessed Incarnate Lord Jesus. Xulon Press, Maitland, FL 2011
    Winners, Losers and Survivors: *Memoir*: Life & Times of Appavoos: 1650-2010 Printed by: Instant Copy & Print. Delta BC 2010
Attridge, Harold W. *Josephus and his Works* Clement of Alexandria AD 190 – 215. cited in E. Goodspeed. *A History f Early Christian Literature*. U of Chicago 1966. p.132
Baggley, John. *Doors of Perception*: Icons of significance. Vladimir Press, N.Y. 1988
Baily, Martin & Doug Gilbert. *The Steps of Bonhoeffer*. Macmillan, New York 1969
Brownrigg, Ronald. *The Twelve Apostles*. Macmillan, New York 1974
Bruce, F. F. *Atlas of the Bible:* The Holy Lands from 2000 BC to Present. Halo Press '95
Clement of Rome. referred to in Eusebius, cited in Schaff p.332
Clement of Rome AD 185 – AD 254 cited in Schaff
Cohen, Shaye J. D. *Josephus in Galilee and Rome*. p.181
Crossan, John Dominic. *The Birth of Christianity*. Harper San Francisco 1998

Daniel-Rops. *Jesus and His Times*. Image Books. Doubleday. New York 1958

Dix, Dom Gregory. *Jurisdiction in the Early Church*: Episcopal and Papal. Faith House, London, 1975

Edersheim, Alfred. *The Life and Times of Jesus the Messiah* v.2 Longmans, London 1884

Eusebius. *History of the Church from AD1 to AD324*. Hendrickson, Mass 4th Printing 2004

Farrar, Frederic W. *The Early Days of Christianity*. Cassell, London 1882

Faye, Elliott. *The Fifth Gospel*. ed. Prentice-Hall, Jerusalem 1972

Gibbon, Edward. *The Decline and fall of the Roman Empire v.1*

Godfrey, F.M. *Christ and the Apostles*: Changing forms of religious Imagery. GB 1957

Goodspeed, Edgar J. *A History of Early Christian Literature*. Revised and enlarged by Robert M Grant. University of Chicago Press 1966

Grabar, von Andre. *Die Mittelalterliche Kunst Osteuropas* Holle Verlag Baden-Baden 70

Green, Michael. *Evangelism in the Early Church*. Hodder and Stoughton, London 1978

Hamm, Dennis. *The Acts of the Apostles*. Liturgical Press, Collegeville, Minnesota 2005

Heritage, Andrew. *Essential World Atlas* 2nd ed. Darling Kindersley Cartography 2001

Ignatius of Rome cited in Schaff p.494

Iranaeus of Lyon quoted in Eusebius, cited in Philip Schaff

Josephus, Flavius. *The Works of Josephus*. New updated edition. Hendrickson 1987

Jurgens, William A. *The Faith of the early Fathers*. v.1 Liturgical Press Collegeville,'70

Justin, Martyr. *Dialogue with the Jew Trypho* c. AD115; *Against All Heresies* c. AD138

Kelly, J.N.D. *Early Christian Doctrines* Revised edition, Harper, N.Y. 1978

Kidd, B. J. *A History of the Church to AD 461.* Clarendon Press, Oxford, 1922 v.1

—*A History of the Church to AD 313.* Oxford 1922

King, Peter. *An Inquiry into the Constitution, Discipline and Worship of the Primitive Church.* Lane & Scott, New York, NY 1851

Madauss, M Martyria. *Jesus a portrait of Love.* Sisterhood of Mary, Darmstadt 1973

Meeks, Wayne. *The First urban Christian*: The Social World of the Apostle Paul. 1983

Menen, Aubrey. *Upon This Rock.* Saturday review Press, New York 1972

Millman. *History of the Jews 1862* Revised edition, cited in Philip Schaff p. 388

Papais, Bishop of Hierapolis in Asia Minor

Pax, Wolfgang. *In the Footsteps of Jesus.* Steimatzky's Agency, Jerusalem 1975

Philip, *An apostle and administrator of alms giving at Jerusalem*: *Acts of Philip; Second Acts refer to period in Athens*

Philo. *The Works of Philo.* Complete and unabridged new and updated ed. Hendrickson 1993

Schaff, Philip. *History of the Christian Church.* v. 1 *Apostolic Christianity*: From the Birth of Christ to the Death of John. Hendrickson. Mass 4th printing 2004

  Nicene & Post-Nicene Fathers. v.1 Eusebius: Church History: Life of Constantine

Simon, Zealot. and Judas Thaddeus worked together hence considered as same person

Sparks, H.F.D. *The Formation of the New Testament.* SCM Press London 1952

Stanley, Dean. *Sermons and essays on the Apostolic Age.* 3rd ed. In Schaff 18?? p.422

Stark, Rodney. *The Rise of Christianity:* A Sociologist Reconsiders history. 1996

Tacitus, Cornelius. *Annals*.15.44 cited in Crossan 1998

Tenney, Merrill C. *The Zondervan Pictorial Bible Dictionary.* Zondervan Publish 1963

Tertullianus, Quintius Septimus. *To the Heathen.* 2vv. AD 197

Wand, J.W.C. *A History of Early Church to AD500.* Methuen, London 3rd ed. 1949

Ward, Baldwin. *Year: Pictorial History of the Bible and Christianity.* New York 1952

The above bibliography was based on the citations referred to in the monographs and edited volumes read by the author. The material were provided by Father Hyndman from the Old Catholic Society, Library of the Oratory of Our Lady of the Nativity in Port Kells, Surrey, BC